MEMORIES

of a

LUCKY
MAN

Phillips Wylly

"Memories of a Lucky Man," by Phillips Wylly. ISBN 978-1-62137-648-4 (hardcover).

Library of Congress Control Number on file with publisher.

Published 2015 by Virtualbookworm.com Publishing Inc., P.O. Box 9949, College Station, TX 77842, US. ©2015, Phillips Wylly. All rights reserved. No part of this publication may be reproduced, stored in a retrieval system, or transmitted in any form or by any means, electronic, mechanical, recording or otherwise, without the prior written permission of Phillips Wylly.

Manufactured in the United States of America.

Dedicated

To my three sons: Phillips, Jr., Christopher Spalding, and David Hamer, who probably wondered where I was and what I was doing while they were growing up.

To their loving mother, Ruth; my wife of 32 years. May she rest in peace.

To my wife, Shirley, who's love means everything to me.

And to Arlene.

"The time has come," the Walrus said,
"To speak of many things.
Of Shoes and Ships and Sealing-wax
And Cabbages and Kings."

Lewis Carroll -1872

Operation Teapot—1955

APRIL 28, 1955—I was in Las Vegas playing cards with Bing Crosby. Well, that may be stretching it a bit. I was sitting at a Black Jack table in the Sands Hotel Casino playing 21 when a man sat down next to me. Concentrating on the ace and six I had in my hand I did not look at him. The dealer had a king showing—what to do. Generally it is a good idea to stand on 17, but when the dealer has a face card showing nine times out of ten he will have another one in the hole, so I decided to take a "hit." I am older and wiser now. Today I never take a card when I have seventeen. The only way such a hand can be improved is with a two, three or four. Anything else and you have lost ground. But what-a-ya think? Call it "beginners luck," I got a Jack. No improvement, but I still had 17.

The dealer turned over his hole card—he had a six, total 16. Less than 17 the dealer must draw. He did—a ten. Bust! I won.

The man seated next to me put down a bet, a silver dollar just like me. (In those glorious days of old real silver dollars were used in Las Vegas then somebody in some federal agency decided it was illegal to use real money so real money was exchanged for plastic chips.) As the man next to me placed his bet I noticed two things: first, underneath his single silver dollar was a carefully folded bill. Second, the man was Bing Crosby. I realize few people reading this today will recognize the name Bing Crosby, but back in those days singer/actor Bing Crosby was perhaps the most popular radio, recording and movie star in the world. Sitting next to him was a big moment for me. Before I got up enough nerve to say something clever, something like "Gee, Mister Crosby, hello," the dealer placed new cards in front of us. I had twenty-one—Black-Jack! (Black Jack, paid two to one in those days and cocktails were free.) Bing had a five showing and, as it turned out, a three in the hole. The dealer had a seven showing; Bing took a card—a Queen as I remember—it gave him eighteen. The dealer had another seven in the hole—fourteen. He took another card—a six. It gave him twenty. Bing stood up and left the table. As he walked away I think he may have said "shit!" but I'm not sure. I was busy collecting my winnings and watching the dealer unfold the bill from under Bing Crosby's silver dollar. It was a one hundred dollar bill.

So what was I doing in Las Vegas? I was there for an A- Bomb Test. Yes, "A-Bomb" as in Atomic Bomb!

During the 1950ies, unaware of, or unconcerned about the dangers of radiation, the Department of Defense was eagerly conducting atomic bomb tests at Frenchman's Flats and several other locations in the Nevada desert. "Operation Teapot," as the then current series was named, had scheduled "Apple-2 a Civil Defense Test" for April 27th.

For Apple-2 a small village named "Survival Town" had been constructed in the Nevada desert some 60 miles away from Las Vegas. With charming houses, small town stores and shops and offices, Survival Town had a population of manikins dressed as men, women and children, including a barber shop with a manikin barber giving a shave to a manikin customer, and a manikin dog sniffing at a real fire hydrant. Survival Town was built in order to study the effects of the blast of a 31-kiloton atomic bomb on a typical American village. Reporters and news-film crews as well as a Hollywood Movie Company had been invited to witness and photograph the test.

I had arrived in Vegas on April 24th, checked into The Sands Hotel and met a film crew from NBC Los Angeles. Together we scouted Survival Town on the 25th and 26$^{th.}$ We traveled up and down the streets filming the houses, buildings and manikin "residents" (including the sniffing dog) then checked out a trench location three miles from blast center from where we would film the explosion. Our camera could be mounted above ground, we were advised, but we must keep our heads below ground level and by no means look at the blast.

April 27th dawned dark and gray. A strong wind was blowing in from the test site towards Las Vegas and rain was in the forecast. The test was scrubbed—re scheduled for the 29th. Come the 29th, more bad weather—another delay. Well, if you are on the expense account, being delayed in Las Vegas is not the worst thing that can happen.

In those days The Sands was the newest and most exciting hotel on "the strip." It was also the hotel furthest out on the strip. Looking to your right as you stepped out the main entrance you could see other hotels, but to the left there was only desert sand surrounding The Sands' lush green grass, shrub, palm tree and swimming pool acreage. I had no interest in wandering around in the desert and there was plenty to do at the Sands. During the day a major attraction was the pool with many more beautiful girls to watch than ever populated the beach back home. And at night—at night The Sands really came alive! Two lavish productions in the main show room—three on Saturday—with headliners such as Martin and Lewis, Frank Sinatra, Liberace and Jimmy Durante. And the Lounge Shows! Three each night, the last one at three or four AM, with name entertainers like the Smothers Brothers, Mort Saul, Louis Prima and Keeley Smith. And, of course, Bing and I could gamble 24 hours a day

I don't remember if they scheduled and canceled another date between April 29th and May 5th, when the test actually happened, but a day or two before the 5th New York called. They wanted me back in NY. Our film of the town and it's "people" was all they really needed, the actual explosion would be covered by the Signal Corps and that footage would be available.

So I missed the big bomb blast.

© San Luis Obispo Tribune

Having an "all expenses" week in Las Vegas certainly qualifies as a "lucky man" memory but I did not appreciate my real luck until 1975 when I read an article about the 20th anniversary of "Apple-2." I was not smart enough to save it, nor do I remember where it was published. I have a sneaky suspicion it was never reprinted and the information contained in it "removed" by some authority. The article reported that of the hundred or more reporters, photographers, and members of a Hollywood Feature Film Company who witnessed the explosion, forty-two had died of cancer within less than twenty years. Checking Google for information about "Operation Teapot" and "Apple-2" the only thing I could find about exposure to radiation was a sentence or

4

two regarding an Atomic Energy Commission report indicating that among the several thousand troops and spectators who participated in those tests a "higher than average number had developed radiation related medical problems."

New York City–1944

FOR MANY YEARS, going back to the silent movie days, the newsreel was an important part of a motion picture theater's entertainment package. Five major companies produced newsreels in this country: RKO Pathe, FOX Movitone, Paramount, Universal, and Hearst Metrotone. In the late 30ies, with World War II on the horizon, newsreels became more and more in demand. By the time war actually began they had become almost essential to an audience anxious to see the devastation wrought by Hitler's hordes and the Allies heroic efforts to stem the German invasions. Newsreels became our windows on a world at war. In many cities theaters devoted to showing only newsreels came into being and as we entered the conflict their number grew and grew.

What happened to newsreels? Paul Alley is what happened to Newsreels. Paul who? I'll get to him in a bit but right now this is all about me.

I was a youngster in 1936 when my family moved from Staten Island, New York, to Port Washington, a lovely small town on Long Island's North Shore. Not long after we got there I met a classmate named Jim Woolley and we became lifelong best friends. Meeting Jim has to go down as perhaps the major lucky event in my life. Lots of reasons for making that statement—I'll probably get to more of them later but for now let me stick with one: Jim's dad was a recording engineer for RKO Pathe News.

In late 1943 our forces were fully engaged in the wars raging in Europe and the South Pacific. Jim and I were seniors in high school, soon to turn 18, soon to be drafted. Then one day, shortly after Thanksgiving, two Army Air Force Recruiters visited Port

Washington High School to tell us seniors how we could join the Air Force, avoid being drafted into the army and not be called for active duty until we graduated in June. Sounded good! The Air Force was exciting! Special! Jim, myself, and a dozen or so others signed up. We were sworn into the Army Air Force Reserve sometime in February, 1944 and excitedly awaited our chance to become Air Force Pilots the following summer. Over the years I have learned that not all things proceed as expected. For me not being called up for active duty in the Army Air Corps was one of those things.

In April, while playing basketball at school, I had a sudden sharp pain in my chest—I could hardly breathe. The school nurse called my mother to have her come get me but mother was not home. I told the nurse I would walk—we did not live far away. I do not know if she really knew what my problem was but I think she was happy at the idea of getting me out of and away from the school. By the time I reached home mother had returned and my pain had grown worse. She immediately telephoned Dr. Newman—our family doctor. In those not so crowded days mother had only to tell the telephone operator, "Doctor Newman please," and she was quickly connected to his office. ("Telephone Operator?" For those of you who are not familiar with the term let me explain. Once upon a time when you picked up the telephone instead of a dial tone a real live, not recorded, female voice asked, "Number Please?" Once you told her the number you wished to call, she placed the call. No dials to twirl, no buttons to push, she did all the work.) In a small town like Port Washington our operators knew by heart the phone numbers for most doctors, a couple groceries and the town's only hardware store.

Within less than half an hour Dr. Newman drove into our driveway and came knocking on our door. (I know you don't believe that. Doctors making house calls? Who am I trying to kid? But cross my heart, it is true. There was such a time.) The doctor quickly determined I had suffered a "Spontaneous Pneumothorax." A collapsed lung caused by a hole in the wall of my lung. "Like a blow-out in an inner tube," Dr. Newman explained. ("Inner Tube." What is an "inner tube" you ask? Well, back in those days of yore an automobile tire did not hold air. A rubber tube was fitted inside the tire and it was this "inner tube" that was inflated. Inner tubes had a propensity to "blow out" and that is what happened to my lung.) Cause? Unknown. Treatment: Bed rest. Prognoses—well there was no way of telling. I am not certain if departing Dr. Newman got all the way out the front door before my mother was on the phone calling the Army Air Force to tell them of my condition. Certainly they would not want anyone with a collapsed lung. Would they? Who knew?

Shortly after graduation that June I was called to an Army Hospital on Governor's Island in New York Harbor where two medical people—nurses? technicians? I don't know, but they listened to my chest, thumped my back and said "hummm" a lot, then they sent me home. No call to active duty.

For some reason during that summer of 1944 Jim Woolley was not called up either. There was nothing wrong with his health, the air force just didn't seem to need either of us quite yet. It was only a matter of time we knew, so enjoy civilian life as long as possible, we told ourselves. And "enjoy" meant just one thing—the beach and all those gorgeous girls!

Our home in Port Washington was located on Beacon Hill. One of the many advantages of living there was access to Beacon Hill Beach, a crescent shaped stretch of sand overlooking Hempstead Harbor. I wish I could say "golden sand" but it wasn't. It was—still is—just sort of... sand color. Never mind the sand, the girls were golden! Some blond, some brunet, at least one red head, all with beautiful golden tan bodies. (In those days of yesteryear the sun was not filtered through all the stuff that is up there now and sun bathing was IN!) Can you think of a better way for an Air Corps headed young man to spend his summer? I can't.

Come September another hospital visit, some more "hummms" but still no call to active duty. Jim too had not been called so we continued to enjoy sunny days at the beach but in September the girls were going back to school so the beach was no longer such a great place to be and one day Jim did not show up. That night I telephoned him—3783, I still remember. (only four numbers in those days.) He told me he had gotten himself a job as an Assistant Film Librarian at RKO Pathe where his father worked. They needed another person in the department, would I like to work there too. "My gosh yes!" I told him. Since I was six years old I had been fascinated with "the movies." The chance to actually work for a company that made movies—newsreels anyway—was a dream come true.

Newsreels of Yesteryear

FOR RKO PATHE, as well as the four other newsreel companies, "Makeup Day" was Monday and Thursday every week. Several thousand feet of film from cameramen all over the world arrived prior to each makeup day. The film editors and writers would view all this film and together decide what stories to use and what scenes to select. The finished newsreel was normally eight to nine minutes long—700 to 800 feet (35mm motion picture film is projected at the rate of 90 feet per minute) which meant there was always a large amount of unused film known as "the cuts."

Several tasks made up the work day of an assistant film librarian. One job was splicing together and labeling "the cuts." Once spliced and labeled this unused film was catalogued and numbered by the female members of the library staff, who were known as "librarians," (Humm—no sex discrimination there.) then placed in fire proof film vaults and made available to production companies that had need for such material. The "fire proof" aspect of those film vaults was very important. In those days 35mm film was nitrate based and extremely flammable. Smoking was absolutely prohibited and fire inspectors checked our vaults, cutting rooms and offices almost weekly.

A second job for the assistant film librarian was to welcome and service people who came to the library in search of material. One searcher was a man named Jim Pozzi, a friendly, "older" man (probably in his early forties) who visited the library several times while I worked there. As I will report a few pages from now meeting and getting to know Jim slightly was very lucky for me.

My life as a Film Librarian was short lived—about seven months long as I remember. I'll get to that but before leaving the library I want to tell you about a member of our Assistant Librarian staff, a remarkable person named George Jorgenson. About my age, George was a pleasant but rather timid young man. I remember Jim Woolley called him "a fag." He told me that one time when they were together in one of the film vaults George actually slapped him in the face because of something he said. I think we all believed George was a "little light in his socks" as we put it. But as it turned out George Jorgenson was also an unbelievably strong, brave and determined person.

Not long after I started to work at Pathe George left. No one knew why he left and I don't suppose any of us really cared very much. It wasn't until some time later that we learned George Jorgenson had gone to Sweden, undergone one of the earliest sex change operations, and become Christen Jorgenson. At the time those of us who had known him laughed and joked about it but as the years have passed I have often thought what courage, what determination it took for him to do that, for him to become the first sex change woman known in this country.

Okay, back to life at Pathe News.

Just after New Year's Day, 1945, Jim Woolley was called to active duty. But not me. Waiting wasn't all that bad, I had a job I loved so what the heck, no rush. Also, I had met a girl named Ruth. Actually during Christmas week Jim and I had met two girls—Betty and Ruth. For a short time I had dated Betty and Jim had dated Ruth but when Christmas week ended Betty went back to school and then Jim was called to active duty. That left Ruth and me in Port Washington. Well, a while after Jim left I called Ruth and asked for a date. (As Steve Allen's 1954 song put it: "This Could Be The Start Of Something Big.")

Come late February, or maybe it was early March, the Army Air Force decided it did not require a Pneumothorax victim. I was discharged and given a small "Ruptured Duck" pin to wear on my lapel to indicate I wasn't a draft dodger, I was officially a veteran free to do as I pleased, free go to college if I wished. But late February was not a time when one entered college. Even if it had been I doubt I would have given college serious thought. From the day I rewound my first reel of film I was hooked. My job at RKO Pathe was a dream come true. Working with film, becoming a Film Editor was the goal of my life. A goal I began moving towards when, shortly after my discharge, I was promoted to Apprentice Film Editor in the Newsreel Editing Room.

Newsreel Makeup Days (Mondays and Thursdays) began at 9AM. As fast as I could fetch film from the laboratory to the "Cutting Room," Assistant Editors would prepare it for viewing, Film Editors and writers would "screen" it, then the editors cut scenes out of the raw footage and assembled them to tell the story. Once the "cut story" was completed a "spot sheet" listing a careful description of each scene and its length was prepared for the writers and music editors. While the writers were writing the music editors would assemble background music, the title department would print and photograph story titles, and the edited footage was sent to the film lab for "work prints," a quickly made positive image to be used for the remainder of the editing process. (The less handling of the original negative the better.)

Once each story's elements were completed and assembled a narrator's voice was recorded and "mixed" with the music department's music. When a satisfactory "take" was accomplished the optical sound track was sent to the film lab for developing. When all this was completed the original picture negative was assembled together with story titles, the developed negative sound track synchronized to the picture negative and the completed newsreel sent to the lab for printing, a process that took about two hours. By two o'clock or so Tuesdays and Fridays mornings the test reel was screened and, if approved, the negative went back to the lab for release printing and shipment to theaters across the country.

And our job was finished. ...Until next Make-Up Day, that is.

New York City—1947

THE SUMMER of 1947 was special for me. In June, on my 21st birthday, Ruth and I announced our engagement. We would be married on August 4th. A week or two after that, sometime in July, I received a surprise phone call from Jim Pozzi—the man I had gotten to know slightly while I was an Assistant Librarian. Jim called to tell me he had just joined NBC Television News as Supervising Film Editor for the new NBC Television Newsreel and ask if I would like to join him as an Assistant Film Editor.

As they say these days, "O!M!G!"

Less than a month away from my wedding day. Was this a time to change jobs? Would it be foolish for me to leave my job at Pathe for something as new and questionable as a television newsreel? Ruth, my bride to be, had a job as a school teacher in Port Washington—soon to reach "tenure," and my job at Pathe seemed secure. We had determined our joint incomes would be enough for us to live on with some degree of comfort. (If I remember correctly I was making $35 a week and Ruth's salary as a teacher in the Port Washington Public School system was $32 a week.) But wow! The chance to move up to Assistant Editor; to move up to a salary of $50 a week??? Wow indeed. Ruth and I talked it over and decided I should seek some advice from the men I worked with.

There were five of us on the Newsreel Film Editing Staff: Harold Bonafield, the Supervising Editor; Film Editor Leonard Heim, First Assistant Editor Albert Helms, Assistant Editor Charlie Morrison and Apprentice Editor, me.

I first consulted Charlie Morrison who told me I was out of my mind. To leave something secure for anything as "iffie" as television I would have to be nuts. Albert had similar thoughts. Leonard agreed with Albert and Charlie and added his belief that television was certainly not going away but what did RCA and NBC know about producing film. If the newsreel idea actually caught on TV Networks would turn to Pathe and the other newsreel companies for such product. I felt my bubble bursting but I wanted to get Harold's thoughts too.

Harold listened to my query, thought for a moment or two then told me, Leonard, Albert and Charlie were right about my job there being secure, he did not think there was much likelihood Pathe would go out of business (a prognosis that turned out to be terribly inaccurate.) He then went on to tell me he expected to retire within fifteen years or so and when he did Leonard would move up to Supervising Editor, Albert would move up to Leonard's job, Charlie to Albert's and I would become the Assistant Editor.

It took me approximately ten seconds to tell Harold I was resigning. Good old Harold rubbed his chin and asked me if I wasn't about to be married and hadn't I put in for my two weeks paid vacation for our honeymoon. Yes, I had. "Then," Harold suggested, "Why don't you wait until you get back before you resign." He felt sure Jim Pozzi would wait.

Honeymoon over (we spent two wonderful weeks in a cabin on beautiful Lake Winnipesaukee) I returned to Pathe, gave my two week notice and as September 1947 began I went to work at NBC—not in glamorous Radio City but in the far from glamorous Film Center on New York's 10th Avenue.

In 1947 not many people owned TV sets and the sets most people did own were large and heavy and had 7 inch screens—about the size of a post card. Television was in black and white and broadcast over the air just like radio. TV sets had aerials, either "rabbit ears" that sat on top of the set or large roof top antennas strapped to chimneys. Ruth and I did not have a TV set but her parents had a 7 inch screen set for which her sister bought a magnifying glass that stood in front of the post card size screen making it appear a bit larger. It was either there, at her parent's house, or, as with most people, in a neighborhood bar, or standing in the street looking at a set in a store window that we viewed our early television.

Back in those days NBC had three of the most popular shows on TV: The Milton Berle Show on Thursday nights, The Gillette Cavalcade of Sports—boxing from New York's Madison Square Garden at 10PM every Friday night—and at 5PM each evening a children's program their parents could not resist , "Kookla, Fran and Ollie," two puppets—Kookla and Ollie—together with a delightful young woman named Fran. It was into this world of programming that a man named Paul Alley, a news writer for NBC, brought his idea for a nightly Television Newsreel.

NBC management was skeptical. Was it possible? With long hours, theater newsreels were produced only twice a week, a newsreel five nights a week seemed like a large order. Paul insisted it could be done. Theater reels, he pointed out, had to be edited, sound tracks recorded, prints made and shipped to theaters. For TV, thanks to a wonder of technology known as "reverse polarity," negative film could be televised as a "positive" picture, thus eliminating the lengthy lab procedure required in order to turn negative film into positive, and Paul himself could read the script directly "on air" eliminating the need to record an announcer's voice. And more important, a TV newsreel had no need for making and shipping prints. All TV had to do was edit the negative film and go on the air. Paul's logic convinced the network brass such a thing could be accomplished and he got a green light. Very quickly Paul hired Jim Pozzi and several film cameramen.

During the war the Signal Corps had trained literally dozens of combat cameramen who by 1947 were looking for work. Paul started with three cameramen in New York, one in Washington DC, one in Chicago and several "stringers" who would be available "on call" in cities like Boston, Cleveland, Detroit and Los Angeles. In addition to film from these sources Paul arranged for film from the Signal Corps and similar European sources.

As Paul was finding cameramen, Jim Pozzi was assembling an editing staff. When I joined the editing crew consisted of Jim himself, another editor named Bob Jacks and me. Within a couple of weeks a third editor, Arthur Rosenblum, was added (Art and I have been close friends ever since.) along with another assistant editor.

I still think meeting Jim Woolley was as the luckiest thing that ever happened to me but joining NBC has to be number two. (Had it not been for Jim I would not have been at Pathe News and would have met Jim Pozzi.) In 1947 television was like a pot that had been on the stove for a while and suddenly began to boil. Wonderful things were happening and opportunity was everywhere. Paul Alley's newsreel was an immediate success and soon air time was extend from ten to fifteen minutes each night. More time meant more stories, more stories required more editors and not long after joining NBC I became an editor.

NBC Television News' fifteen minute program at 7PM each night quickly grew to 30 minutes (Monday through Friday) and Paul Alley's organization grew as well. Within a year after I joined the staff had more than tripled.

Phillips Wylly

This is
NBC NEWSREEL

Simon Avnet has the determined look of a man making a "scoop," as he steadies his tripod to shoot.

Cameraman Tom Burney checks distance and focus for an angle shot, from a high vantage point.

News Editor Jesse Sabin looks over current AP wire reports.

Jim Pozzi, Cutting Room Editor, reviews a reel at the Moviola.

Art Rosenblum beside the film barrel, with Gerald Polikoff.

Librarian Fran Kerwin and Henry Ferens file for future reference.

Jim Woolley wields his brush carefully as he splices chosen footages.

Editor-in-Chief Paul Alley reads his script against a stopwatch.

Traffic Manager Johnny Krumpelbeck and the reels for the day.

Office Manager Stan Rotkewicz and Frank Baker check routings.

Film Editor Phil Wylly selects shots, Asst. Ken Baldwin watching.

Mme. Chiang Kai-shek, as she appeared in a recent NBC reel.

The smiling cameraman is Joe Vadala, whose films covering Washington and the near South for the Newsreel are flown to New York.

Yes the fellow on the splicer (middle picture left hand row) is Jim Woolley. Jim had been discharged from the Air Corps and re-started his career in the film world. And yes, editor Arthur Rosenblum is the very close friend of whom I wrote.

Not long after NBC Chimes published this page of pictures of Paul Alley and his staff, in 1948 Paul's half-hour TV Newsreel became "The Camel News Caravan," with personable, good looking John Cameron Swazey as on air host and commentator.

17

Great news for everyone but Paul Alley who was not a Lucky Man. Paul was neither handsome nor particularly TV personable and he suddenly found himself replaced—out of a job. (Don't let anyone tell you life in the TV world is always kind.)

Among the team of new writers who took over for Paul were two newspaper men who went on to great things. The first was Gerry Green. Gerry became the first producer of "Today" and published his first novel, "The Last Angry Man," a few years later. (1956) A movie made from Gerry's novel, staring Paul Muni, won several Academy Awards.

Gerry was a friend while we worked together on the "Camel News Caravan."

A second new writer, Reuven Frank, joined us at about the same time. Reuven spent the rest of his career at NBC eventually becoming the President of NBC News. We also became friends and, as I will relate later, I worked for him while he was producing major documentaries for the network.

The Man Who Changed the World

In 1949 Sylvester "Pat" Weaver became President of NBC and began to revolutionize television.

As the TV network expanded in '48 and '49 television audiences grew and so did sponsor demand for air time. In those days of yore the television year was divided into two segments: 39 weeks of "prime time" (Early September to Early June) and 13 weeks of summer doldrums—re-runs and inexpensive programming. Major sponsors bought the 39 weeks of prime time but many took the summers off. One such sponsor was Gillette—the razor blade manufacturer. As I wrote earlier, Friday night's Gillette Cavalcade of Sports was a big hit in those golden days of television. It made money for NBC and, perhaps more important, it drew audiences to the network. Even more important, it sold razor blades. But by 1950 competition for prime time had reached a point where Pat Weaver decided NBC could go to its sponsors and tell them if they wished to keep the same program time next fall they would have to buy the time for the 13 summer weeks as well. Gillette said okay but what could they program? They were identified with boxing and there was no boxing in the summer. Someone at NBC said Gillette should be identified with all sports and suggested a weekly filmed sports review. The idea worked for Gillette. Worked for me too because guess what, I had always been interested in sports. When newsreel coverage of a ball game or a ski jump or a tennis match came in I was usually the guy who "cut" the story so who more logical than me for the job of Supervising Film Editor for the Gillette Sports Review which began its 13 week life just after Memorial Day 1950. And by gosh it got good ratings at 10 PM each Friday night.

In 1950 the co-axial cable reached only a few major cities—more were being added all the time but for much of the country Network TV was only seen via rather poor quality "kinescope," a 16mm film photographed off a TV screen in the studio. The best quality TV in the non-cable world was either local programming or high quality motion picture film. The idea of being able to present a filmed sports review to all those non cable outlets was an opportunity Gillette wanted to explore. So our thirteen week baby grew into a fifty-two weeks a year production and I found myself spending a lot of time outside the cutting room directing cameramen who were not all that familiar with sporting events.

Okay, back to Pat Weaver:

Shortly after assuming the presidency he created "Broadway Open House," an hour long, live comedy show staring Jerry Lester and (later) a blond bombshell named Dagmar. The show was presented nightly (Monday to Friday) from 11pm to midnight. Who was he kidding? Who was going to stay up watching TV until midnight? As it turned out a lot of people did. After a while "Broadway Open House" became the "Tonight" show with Steve Allen then Jack Par then Johnny Carson, etc. etc.

Weaver's next new idea was the "Today" show. He believed if people would watch TV until midnight there was no reason why they would not watch it at seven o'clock in the morning. (A lot of people thought that idea was pretty far out—I was one of them.) With Gerry Green as producer, "Today" went on the air in 1952 and you know, like "Tonight", it is still going strong more than sixty years later.

Something worth remembering about those early days of television is the creative talent involved and the tremendous number of great shows offered as opposed to today's plethora of police shoot-em-ups and amature hours. The reason for that, in large measure, is because in those golden days federal law prohibited any one company from owning more than five television stations. The remainder of the "network" was made up of independent stations who became "affiliates," and carried the network's programming. The more affiliates a network had, the more it could charge for commercial time. To attract affiliates a network had to have programming that attracted the largest number of viewers.

So what has all this history got to do with me? Quite a bit actually. I have reported my great luck in landing the Gillette show but nothing lasts forever…well, maybe some things do—"Today" for example—but not the Gillette Sports Review. It closed down as the prime time season began in September, 1952. Almost immediately after that Gerry Green offered me a chance to head up the film editing staff for the brand new early morning Weaver creation. Seven o'clock in the morning? I didn't think so. I didn't think a show at that time of day could draw an audience. (I also didn't think we could land a man on the moon or elect a black president.) But you know what? That decision was a lucky one for me because a few months after "Today" hit the airwaves another Weaver creation came along. "HOME." A day time "magazine format" show intended to attract a women's audience.

In the fall of 1952 a unique set was being constructed for "HOME" on the grounds of an old horse stable at Columbus Circle in New York City. Round in shape, the set was divided into pie slice, wedge shape "sets" for the various segments of the show. The cooking wedge would be complete with a full kitchen and presided over by Cooking Editor, Master Chef Poppy Cannon; Sewing Editor Nancy Ann Graham's wedge would boast a sewing machine and an ironing board; the top soil filled gardening wedge would be ready for anything Gardening Editor Will Piggleback cared to plant, Estelle Parsons presided over another wedge. (A side note here: A 2014 Tony Awards nomination for Best Actress went to Estelle. Seeing her brief appearance on TV persuaded me to try and contact her. Guess what? We have reconnected after all these years.) Okay, you get the idea, there would be a wedge for fashions, a wedge for health care, and a double size wedge from where announcer/co-host Hugh Downs and the Editor in Chief/Hostess would introduce show segments, interview guests and generally conduct the daily program.

Arlene Francis was selected for the Editor in Chief/Hostess job

Arlene Francis was in her early 40ies when she ventured into television. She had been a moderately successful actress in films and on Broadway but became a true celebrity as a member of the "What's My Line?" panel. From 1950 until 1967 "What's My Line" was the top rated Sunday evening TV show. The panelists would question contestants from various walks of life and try to determine what their profession was. The contestants had only to answer "Yes," or "No," to their questions. If the panel could not guess it correctly with no more than ten questions, the contestant won.

The most audience enjoyable "contestant" each week was the "Mystery Guest," A famous celebrity, instantly recognizable by audience and panel members, thus the panel wore masks covering their eyes while trying to determine who the Mystery Guest was. It was during the hay-day of "What's My Line" that Arlen Francis came to HOME.

It had not been intended for HOME to ever go outside the fabulous studio being built for it, but as 1953 "Show Time" approached HOME's first producer, Jack Rayle began to think that maybe, just maybe, once in a while there might be a time when something outside the studio would be of interest to the audience. Maybe a guest's house, maybe a favorite tree with a swing where the guest entertained his or her children or grandchildren, maybe the beach a future guest would like to reminisce about. (No, not Beacon Hill Beach—well, maybe?) Who could guess? However it might be good to have that capability, Jack thought. But hey, location work? Back in those days TV Remote units were few and far between. They were big, bulky, difficult to move and set up, expensive to operate and video tape did not exist. Even a fair haired new show like HOME had a budget so TV remotes were not practical, but newsreel type film cameras, with a one or two man crew, were easy. Better look into this, Jack told himself.

With the weekly sports review gone I was more or less treading water when our news department boss told me about HOME and

Jack Rayle's interest in having someone on board who could handle small film projects. Would I be interested? Yes, I certainly would. (I had turned down "Today." Confucius say not wise to turn down too many chances!)

A few blocks away from the still under construction HOME studio at Columbus Circle the second floor of the Dauphin Hotel, at Broadway and 67th Street, housed HOME's production staff. It was there that I met Jack Rayle. (Jack, if you happen to be reading this I'm sorry if I have miss-spelled your name. I may have forgotten the correct spelling but I shall never forget you. I have no idea what my life might have been without your help.)

"We probably will not use more than a couple of minutes of film each week," Jack Rayle told me, (a prediction that turned out to be far from accurate) "But it could be from anywhere in the country. I know you have been working with cameramen all over the place so it should be right down your alley, What-a-ya-think?"

"Will Monday be soon enough for me to start?" I answered.

HOME went on the air in the Spring of 1953 and was a daily audience pleaser until the summer of 1957. During those four years Jack Rayle's predicted "couple of minutes" of film from outside the studio became five or ten minutes a day and my adventures as the producer and director of HOME's film elements were almost unbelievable.

Dinner with Jackie

NOT LONG after HOME went on the air one of our writers came up with an idea for a recurring segment to be titled "At HOME With." The basic premise was to introduce our audience to the real person behind a famous name. I like to think the success of our early film segments had something to do with this idea in which a well-known person would be Arlene's studio guest to talk of his or her life away from and out of the public eye. To provide visual images of that life, a few days before the studio visit, my film crew and I would go to the subject's home and film her or him in that environment. And then, guess what, some most desirable subjects were unable to come to the studio. Well as the saying goes "if the mountain will not come to Mohamed, Mohamed must go to the mountain." So Arlene Francis joined me and together we went to visit many "guest" in their own homes, where we filmed the entire segment. Such was the case when we were "At HOME with Jackie Kennedy."

Jacqueline Lee Bouvier and Senator John F. Kennedy were married in September, 1953. A year or so later—fall of '54—NBC people in Washington arranged for an "At HOME With" segment with Jackie Kennedy. (I realize now that this "arrangement" was actually the start of John Kennedy's march towards the Democratic Nomination and eventual election as President of the United States.)

Arlene and I flew down to Washington and on the appointed day went to the Kennedy home in Georgetown where we were welcomed by the charming, delightful, beautiful lady who was to be our "At HOME" guest for the day. For the next several hours Mrs. Kennedy gave Arlene and our camera a tour of her home.

24

They talked about this and that—items of furniture, favorite clothes, her life before meeting the Senator. She told of her early years in New York City and East Hampton, on Long Island and of the various schools she had attended. She spoke about her college years—two at Vassar followed by two in France, one at the University of Grenoble and one at the Sorbonne. At Arlene's prompting, she talked about her debut in 1947 when columnist Igor Cassini's labeled her "Debutante of the Year."

She told us of her first job as an "Inquiring Photographer" for the Washington Times Herald and of covering the first inauguration of Dwight D. Eisenhower and the coronation of Queen Elizabeth II and smiled when Arlene asked about the story that she had met her handsome husband to be at a dinner party where, supposedly, "he leaned across the asparagus and asked her for a date."

"Well," she laughed, "I'm not sure it was the asparagus."

They were married a year later, on September 12, 1953.

The Kennedy home was large, comfortable and had what I would call a sunken living room; it was a step, maybe two steps below the front entrance hallway. About four o'clock, maybe closer to five, we were set up in the living room when the Senator appeared in the hallway. John F. Kennedy was a very imposing man under any circumstances but his sudden, unexpected arrival, coupled with the fact that he was standing a foot or so above us, made for a moment of surprise and awe. Mrs. Kennedy quickly introduced us as he stepped down into the living room; he was warm, charming, cordial. He was very sorry he could not stay and take part in the filming but he was already late for a dinner meeting. He gave his wife a quick kiss, told her he would not be home until quite late and was gone almost before he had arrived.

An hour or so later we completed our work and were getting ready to leave. Arlene and I started thinking about dinner and where to eat. "Jackie," as we were calling her by then, suggested a restaurant. Something about her attitude, her tone of voice, maybe her "look,"—something made me think that since her husband would not be home, she might like to have dinner with us. I mentioned this to Arlene who quickly turned to Jackie. "With your husband gone for the evening, what are you doing about dinner?" Arlene asked. "Nothing," Jackie answered. "Well why don't you have dinner with us?"

Although we were welcomed like the celebrities Jackie and Arlene truly were, I don't remember the restaurant's name nor what we ate; nor do I remember much of our "small talk" conversation. What I do remember is, toward the end of the evening, there was a look on Jackie's face as she thanked us and told us how she loved to go out for dinner and this night was special for her because Jack was away so much and she was so often alone.

I saw that "look" on Jacqueline Kennedy's face once again, many years later as she and her two young children stood watching the parade and her husband' coffin passing by. My feeling was, and is still today, that behind the glamour and charm that made people think she was the ultimate fairy princess there was a woman whose life was perhaps not all she had expected and hoped it would be.

A Lonely Man

ROCKY GRAZIANO (1 January 1919 – May 22, 1990) born
Thomas Rocco Barbella *in New York City was an American boxer. Graziano was considered one of the greatest knockout artists in boxing history, often displaying the capacity to take his opponent out with a single punch. He was ranked 23rd on Ring Magazine's list of the greatest punchers of all time. Graziano's life story was the basis of the 1956 Academy Award winning film "Somebody Up There Likes Me." based on Graziano's 1955 autobiography of the same title. The film starred Paul Newman and was directed by Robert Wise.*

Far be it for me to correct the internet but I don't think "Somebody Up There Likes Me" won the Oscar in 1956. It was nominated but it did not win. But that is beside the point. It was a good film and it was based on the book written by Rocky Graziano.

Not long after the book was released an agent contacted HOME about doing a story on Rocky. HOME was always looking for material and a literary boxer who's book was beginning to draw critical praise seemed an interesting guest for the show. "Sure," said the powers that be. "We can do an 'At Home With' segment?"

"Ahhh, well…. 'At Home' might not be possible. Rocky's wife might not go for that."

"So, okay, he can come to the studio, Arlene will interview him here."

"Ahhh, well… Rocky isn't into studios. How 'bout maybe you could interview him here in my office?"

I don't know exactly how all that went down but on a Tuesday afternoon, at about 1:30, I arrived at the agent's office where a film crew was to meet me. Arlene would join us at 2 o'clock as would Rocky Graziano.

But this was one of those days when everything got fucked up! First of all, Rocky was already there when I arrived, had been for half an hour or so.

But no film crew. That didn't concern me too much, they were not due until 2 o'clock and it was only 1:30. I knew the guys would be there soon and it gave me a chance to chat with Rocky Graziano! As I have reported, before HOME I worked on the Gillette Sports show. I was very familiar with Rocky's career and excited to have a chance to get to know him.

In no time 2PM rolled around but still no film crew and no Arlene. I apologized to Rocky. Our planned schedule was to shoot from 2 o'clock to 4 o'clock. Obviously we were going to be late. Rocky told me not to worry.

I made a couple of phone calls. The crew was now on the way—they had a flat tire on Madison Avenue at 88th Street. Okay. But where was Arlene? She had never been late for anything in her life. Could something have happened to her? The answer arrived just as I was making another phone call: Sy Avnet, our cameraman, holding the office door open for Arlene.

"That was the worst cab ride I ever had!" It was the closest I ever saw Arlene come to anger.

"Tell me your troubles," Sy laughed. "We had a flat tire on Madison Avenue."

While Sy and the boys got set up Arlene and Rocky became like old friends and soon we were ready to roll. But it was to be an afternoon made in hell. Five minutes in the film broke. Now film does not break in a camera. It just damn well doesn't! But it did. Something in the Mitchell Camera was not right.

So, they fixed it.

It was well after five o'clock when we finally finished. Arlene had to dash away for another appointment and I was hoarse from apologizing to Rocky but he seemed to be perfectly okay with everything. I asked him if I could buy him a drink. He said that would be great and we went to "The King Cole Room" in a hotel just down the street. Now imagine, will you, me sitting in The King Cole Room having a drink with a World Champion boxer. I lifted my glass, tilted it towards him and said once again, "Rocky, I'm truly sorry we fucked up your afternoon."

He tipped his glass towards me and said, "Lem-me tell ya something."

Today, almost sixty years later, I can still remember his words.

"Ya know how I talk…" Rocky said. (He had a lower east side street gang "dem" and "dose" dialect.) "Me an my wife, we got two daugh-tuz an she don't like dem hearin' da way I talk. She's afraid dey might start talkin' like me so she don't wan me hangin' 'roun-da house. So I go out. I use-ta go down ta-da gym. But dere was aways some new kid workin' out an somebody always want me ta-spar wid him. So, I get in da ring and da kid's a box-a, you know what I mean, an-I ain't neva been no box-a, so afta he pops me a couple-a times I hit him. Dat's what I do. I knock the kid down and everybody says I should-en be so rough on da kid. So I don go ta-da gym no more."

He paused, looked at the drink he was holding in his hand and nodded his head up and down once or twice. "So I started goin at-da movies," he said slowly "I seen every movie on 42nd Street at least twice. Phil, I ain't got nutten ta -do. Dis afternoon wid you and Arlene and da guys was the most fun I had in weeks." We sat quietly for a minute or two, sipping our drinks, then Rocky looked at his wrist watch, "Da goils ought-a be in bed by now," he told me. "I guess I can go home."

Short Subjects:

Eggs ala Wolfe

Rex Todhunter Stout (December 1, 1886 – October 27, 1975) was an American writer best known as the creator of Nero Wolfe, a greatly over weight detective who seldom left his New York house full of orchids. Nero Wolfe did most of his detecting by sorting through the material his "leg man" and loyal assistant Archie Goodwin uncovered. From 1934 until Stout's death in 1975 Nero Wolfe novels were best sellers. Several were made into movies and a Nero Wolfe TV series was popular during the 1950ies. Stout wrote countless books, received many awards and was widely acclaimed as the best mystery writer in America. Some day when you are in the library give Nero Wolfe a shot. (I know, I know, Library? What's that? Okay, check it out on Amazon.)

I don't remember the date but one day the film crew and I traveled to Danbury, Connecticut to film Rex Stout at home. The film we would take would be used a few days later when he would be Arlene's in studio "At Home With," guest. Stout had to be nearly 70 years old but one would never guess it. I thought he was about fifty. Nero Wolfe, his fictional hero, was grossly overweight; Stout himself was in great physical shape. He loved to work in his yard and he loved to cook. After showing off his gardens he invited us to have a special lunch with him: "Eggs ala Wolfe."

We set up our camera in his kitchen and photographed his culinary efforts:

Into a large frying pan he placed a pound of bacon, separated the strips as the bacon cooked then carefully removed each strip and placed it on a brown paper bag to drain. As he removed the strips of bacon from the frying pan he was careful to let the fat drip back into the pan. With all the bacon removed there was a nearly half inch deep pool of bacon drippings in the pan. Stout then carefully poured in about a half cup of vinegar, added a couple of tea spoons full of fresh ground pepper, waited a minute or so for the bacon fat to return to a near boiling temperature then added the eggs. I try to crack eggs once in a while but at least one out of three times I break the yoke, not Rex Stout. With a flourish, he opened a full dozen eggs without breaking a single yoke. That impressed me!

"Eggs ala Wolfe" was delicious! But how any one could eat them more than once a month without gaining a hundred pounds is beyond me.

Well, he didn't say how often he ate them.

Them There Eyes

(Pinckard, Tuber & Tracey—1930)

For more than 20 years, 1938 to 1959, Rise Stevens was the Metropolitan Opera's star mezzo-soprano and got top billing, a position usually awarded to the tenor or soprano. In her nearly quarter-century with the Met, Ms. Stevens was most famous for Bizet's "Carmen." She sang the title role 124 times with the company. She also appeared on Broadway, television, movies and toured the concert world.

The daughter of a Norwegian-born father and an American mother, Rise Gus Steenberg was born on June 11, 1913, in the Bronx, New York, and reared in a railroad apartment there. (Her given name is pronounced REE-suh; her middle name was after an aunt, Augusta.)

As a young girl she earned a dollar a week singing on "The Children's Hour," a Sunday morning program on the local radio station WJZ. She took the professional name Rise Stevens as a teenager.

She was married for 61 years to the same man, Walter Surovy, which must be a record for any entertainment personality. She died in 2013, just three months short of her one hundredth birthday. Another record for entertainment world personalities. She and her husband had one son, Nicolas, who became an actor on Broadway and in films.

During the years HOME was on the air, when Rise Stevens was perhaps at the top of her career, she agreed to be an "At HOME With" guest. Several days before her scheduled studio appearance, together with a film crew, I went to the large, but not overly so, comfortable New York apartment where she lived to film material for her and Arlene to talk about. I confess I had not done much homework regarding Rise Stevens. I had seen her in the Bing Crosby film "Going My Way," I had heard some of her recordings and seen her on Ed Sullivan's TV Show several times, but I had been unaware of her age or family status.

I do not remember specifically what we took pictures of—the usual bits of memorabilia, a favorite chair, a picture, the piano at which she practiced every day, pictures of her husband and young son. (I had been unaware she was married. I believe husband and son were at their more permanent home in Connecticut.)

Rise Stevens was a remarkable talent, a warm, engaging personality and a very beautiful lady in every sense of the word. She also had the most sparkling eyes I have ever seen. I was mesmerized by her eyes, I was intrigued by her eyes. I was fascinated by her eyes. As the lyrics of the Pinckard, Tauber and Tracey song proclaimed, "They sparkle, they bubble, the could get you in a whole lot of trouble."

So, I spent a wonderful day with a charming, delightful woman who made me feel as though I were someone special. End of story? Well, not quite. For the end of this story we must jump ahead some 40 years.

I was in Buenos Aries with Robert Duval making the a film, "The Man Who Captured Eichmann." for TNT. It was the story of the capture of Adolph Eichmann, a Nazi war criminal, by Mossad, the Israeli secret service. Bob Duval played Eichmann, a group of younger actors played the members of the Mossad team that went to Argentina to find him. One of those actors was Nicolas Surovy. Name ring a bell? It didn't to me at the time but one day when I was going off to look for filming locations "Nick" asked if he could come along. He wanted to see more of Buenos Aries, he had been there as a child. One of the locations I went to look at was the "Colon Theater," Buenos Aries' world famous Opera House. As Nick and I walked out onto the stage he took in a deep breath and said, more or less to himself, "It hasn't changed a bit."

"You've been here before?" I asked him.

"Yes, when I was a child, with my mother. She sang here."

"Oh wow. Who was your mother?"

"Rise Stevens," he told me.

It was my turn to take a deep breath. "Is she still alive? Is she well?' I asked him.

"Oh yeah. She and dad are doing great."

"Well please tell her "hello" from the man who brought the TV HOME Show film crew into her home way back in 1950 something. And tell her, her eyes are still shining bright in my mind.

Another Cook

AS I HAVE MENTIONED more than once, my memory of things that happened many years ago is not as complete as I wish it were. I remember things that were special but not all the details. Case in point, my afternoon with Henry Fonda. Surely everyone recognizes his name. In 1999 the American Film Institute named him "Sixth Greatest Male Star of All Time." (Who were the first five? Don't ask!)

Fonda was born in Grand Island, Nebraska, in 1905 but did not begin acting until he was 20 when a friend of his mother's suggested he try out for a part in a production being put on by the Omaha Community Playhouse. Believe it or not his mother's friend was a woman named Dodie Brando. Yes, Marlon Brando's mother. (Now don't tell me you don't know who Marlon Brando was.) In 1928 Henry Fonda took a deep breath, crossed his fingers and went to New York with the dream of an acting career. So, you skeptics, some dreams do come true.

The year was probably 1954 when I met Henry Fonda. He and his family were living in a Brownstone in New York City. When this adventure came to mind I thought he was living in New York because he was appearing in the Broadway Play,

"Mr. Roberts;" but checking dates with Wikipedia I learned the play ran from 1948 to 1951. So, he was not in New York for the play. Why was he living there? I have no idea, but he was. And somehow Poppy Cannon learned he was and knew he loved to cook.

Poppy Cannon was a well-known cooking expert who wrote newspaper columns, did radio shows and was HOME's Food Editor. She contacted Henry and persuaded him to be her in studio guest and show off his cooking. Poppy's "wedge" of the HOME studio pie was complete with a full kitchen but Henry would have nothing to do with cooking in a strange kitchen. He would cook, but only in his own kitchen. So, I took a crew to his house on East 50 something street to film him cooking.

Most New York Brownstones look pretty much alike. From the street they have a stairway going up one level to the formal front door; alongside that stairway, two or three steps lead down to a separate door that, in the case of Henry's house, led directly into a pantry and the kitchen.

When our equipment van pulled up in front of the house there were three or four young lads roller skating around the entrance. They stood by watching us unload and carry camera and lights into the house.

Once in the kitchen we set up our camera, lit "the set," and Henry began too cook. He had not much more than put a pan on the stove when two of the young boys, sans roller skates, appeared. One was Henry's son Peter. Henry quickly chased them away and turned back to his cooking.

"Take a close-up of the pan as I put in some butter," he directed.

A few more ingredients later Peter and friend re-appeared. "Clear out," Henry told them in no uncertain tones.

In time we finished filming whatever it was he was cooking, packed up our gear and left.

Some twenty years later I was part of David Wolper's production team for a TV Movie titled: "Collision Course: Truman vs. McArthur." E.G. Marshall played President Truman and Henry Fonda was General Douglas MacArthur. During a break in the filming I said hello to Henry, mentioned we had met twenty years earlier when he cooked for the HOME Show. He nodded and said something like, "Oh yeah, I remember." I didn't know if he actually remembered anything about it but I asked him if he still enjoyed cooking.

"Yes, I do," he told me. "And it's a lot better without kids coming in all the time."

Words to Remember

"The only thing we have to fear is fear itself."

President Franklin D. Roosevelt

"Ask not what your country can do for you; ask what you can do for your country."

President John F. Kennedy

"I have a dream..."

Civil Rights Leader Martin Luther King

"Once there were twin brothers; one ran away to sea, the other became Vice President and was never heard from again."

Vice President Albin Barkley

ALBIN BARKLEY was the 35th Vice President of the United States serving under President Harry Truman from 1949 to 1953. Shortly after his term in office ended he was in New York City, living in the Waldorf Towers—the Waldorf Astoria Hotel. Why was he living there? I don't know. He was, however, engaged in a race for a senate seat and had agreed to appear on HOME.

Barkley was born in 1877 in McCracken County, Kentucky. He had a legal degree but spent most of his life in politics as a congressman or senator. He was known for his warm, friendly personality, his great sense of humor and his ability as a powerful speaker.

The 1948 Democratic Convention began as a rather lack luster event. President Truman's roll since President Roosevelt's death had not received wide enthusiasm and the general feeling was that Republican Candidate, Thomas Dewey, was going to be the next president. Step up Key Note Speaker Albin Barkley. Barkley lit a fire in the delegates as well as the voting public and as a result was nominated to be Truman's running mate. Fire or no fire, not many pundits believed a Truman/Barkley ticket could top Tom Dewey's freight train. The pundits were so convinced of a Dewey victory that come election day—actually the morning after—the New York Times first edition headline proclaimed Dewey the winner. A classic photograph from that day shows a grinning, re-elected President Harry Truman holding up a copy of that front page.

Barkley was quickly given the nickname "The Veep" by his grandson and the name stuck with him.

Following our usual format, I took a crew to the Waldorf Towers to film the Vice President at home. He welcomed us in a warm, friendly manor and seemed genuinely pleased to have us there. We set up our lights and began filming. One of the things he liked best about living at the Waldorf, he told us, was the view from his windows. He thought New York was a magical city and loved to look out over it. He showed us some personal things he said he always took with him—family photos, his bible. You know I don't remember much about what we saw and filmed on those "At HOME" visits and this visit was no exception. What I do remember is the warmth and charm of the man. Also I have a very clear memory of two things: the chair in which the Vice President sat had a rather large worn spot in the upholstery of one arm. ("This is the Waldorf Astoria?" I asked myself.)

Second memory, this snap shot of me with the former Vice President of the United States.

Bean Soup

MARGARET CHASE SMITH served in the United States House of Representatives from 1940 to 1949, then as U.S. Senator from Maine from 1949 until 1974. Until then, she was the first woman ever to serve in both houses and was certainly an early leader in what we still seem to call "the women's movement."

Senator Smith was a natural for a women's show like HOME.

I'm not sure which year it was when she agreed to be Arlene's guest on the show, very likely 1954, the year she was running for her second term in the Senate. She could not leave her office and come to the New York Studio so Arlene and I went to Washington and spent several hours with her in her Senate Office as she told Arlene about her early life and entry into politics.

She was born Margaret Madeline Chase, December 14, 1897 in Skowhegan, Maine. Her father was the town barber, and her mother worked as a waitress, store clerk, and shoe factory worker. The Senator told us at age 12, she went to work at a local five-and-dime store and even bought herself a life insurance policy. She also shaved her father's customers when he was busy or away from the shop.

(I remember smiling and rubbing the stubble on my cheek, "I don't suppose...." I said.) The Senator and Arlene gave me a rewarding smile.

She had attended Skowhegan High School, graduating in 1916, she continued. During her high school years she worked as a substitute operator with a telephone company and during that time she met the man who was later to become her husband, Clyde Smith, a prominent local politician, who arranged a job for her as a part-time assistant to the tax assessor. It was the beginning of her life in politics.

Smith and the Senator were married in1930. For several years after they married she served on the Republican State Committee until 1936 when her husband decided to run for the U.S. House of Representatives. After helping with his campaign, once he was elected she became his secretary.

Representative Clyde Smith died of a heart attack in April, 1940, Margaret assumed his position and won a special election that June.

Senator Smith took us to lunch in the Senate Dining Room that day. The Senator, and our very courteous waiter, urged me to try the Navy Bean Soup—a Senate Dining Room Specialty. And, oh my, what a specialty it was. I can almost taste that soup today. I have enjoyed Navy Bean Soup at many restaurants since then but never have I tasted any quite as wonderful. That soup was reason enough to want to be a U.S. Senator. I still have the copy of the menu I took for a souvenir. It has the soup recipe printed on the back:

THE FAMOUS SENATE RESTAURANT BEAN SOUP RECIPE

Take two pounds of small Navy Pea Beans, wash, and run through hot water until Beans are white again. Put on the fire with four quarts of hot water. Then take one and one-half pounds of Smoked Ham Hocks, boil slowly approximately three hours in covered pot. Braise one onion chopped in a little butter, and, when light brown, put in Bean Soup. Season with salt and pepper, then serve. Do not add salt until ready to serve. (Eight persons.).

It was a wonderful lunch, thank you Senator Smith!

The Gazebo

*The fog comes
on little cat feet.
It sits looking
over harbor and city
on silent haunches
and then moves on.*

Carl Sandburg

IT WAS NOT fog that came on "little cat feet," it was his wife tip toeing quietly through the trees that rimmed the large yard to the Gazebo where her husband and Arlene were seated. She did not want to interrupt, she did want to get close enough to hear what they were saying. I tapped cameraman Sy Avnet on the shoulder and gestured to pan the camera over to her while our sound man kept recording Arlene's and her husband's conversation. (Having only one camera does have its limits but this moment was too wonderful to miss.)

We were at Connemara, a 250 acre country estate near Flat Rock, North Carolina, "At HOME" with Pulitzer Prize winning author and poet Carl Sandburg. I do not recall his telling us where the name "Connemara" came from but in 1945 he, his wife and family moved there and lived there until his death in 1967.

Connemara was a large, unpretentious farm house surrounded by fields of ripening corn and acres of woodland. We were welcomed like old friends.

Mrs. Sandburg and their daughter prepared a great lunch for us all. Following lunch, she shooed us out of the house and to the gazebo in the yard behind where, while she and daughter did the dishes, Sandburg and Arlene could talk about his life:

Born July 6,1878, into a family of modest means in Galesburg, Illinois, Carl Sandburg dropped out of school at age 13 and began driving a milk wagon. Several years later he became a porter at the Union Hotel in Galesburg for several years before leaving home to go to Kansas where he became a brick layer and farm worker. In 1898 the Spanish/American War found him in the army and following that he attempted West Point but failing a test in Grammar he did not qualify. Shortly after that a job as a reporter for the Chicago News was the beginning of his writing career. When we visited him he may have become a North Carolinian but his work and his image will always be those of a mid-westerner.

Sandburg's first Pulitzer Prize, for History, came in 1940 for "Abraham Lincoln, The War Years." A second Pulitzer for poetry followed in 1951. An example of how the past sometimes predicts the future, in 1974, while I was with David Wolper's company, we produced a mini-series titled "Carl Sandburg's Lincoln." Hal Holbrook (who spent hours in make-up each day) played President Lincoln.

Carl Sandberg was an icon.. The opportunity to meet him was so meaningful to our Producer, Ted Rogers, and writer, Gene Wycoff, that they both traveled to Flat Rock with Arlene, me, and our film crew to do so.

Left to Right: Arlene Francis, Sandberg's Daughter (standing), Carl Sandberg, Mrs Sandberg, Me, Writer Gene Wycoff, Producer Ted Rogers

A final Sandburg note: He was a strong supporter of Civil Rights and was the first white man to be honored by the NAACP with their Silver Plaque Award, proclaiming him "a major prophet of civil rights in our time."

Carl Sandburg was a great man. Meeting him was indeed an honor!

He died July 22, 1967

O God, there's noises I'm going to be hungry for.
Good-by now to the streets and the clash of wheels and
locking hubs,
The sun coming on the brass buckles and harness knobs.
The muscles of the horses sliding under their heavy
haunches,
Good-by now to the traffic policeman and his whistle,
The smash of the iron hoof on the stones,
All the crazy wonderful slamming roar of the street.-

Carl Sandburg

God Bless America

ACCORDING TO WIKIPEDA: "**God Bless America**" is an American patriotic song written by Irving Berlin in 1918 and revised by him in 1938 for Kate Smith. For a time she had exclusive right to perform the song which became her signature song and our unofficial National Anthem during World War 2.

Kate Smith is an American Music legend.

To promote her new NBC TV show Arlene and I spent a day "At Home" with her. The idea of our visit was Kate had invited Arlene to lunch at her home somewhere in Connecticut. Back in those ancient days the Teamsters Union did not completely control all vehicular movement so the film crew drove themselves to Kate's home in one car and I drove Arlene and myself in another.

Checking good old Wikipedia again I find information indicating Kate Smith had a home at Lake Placid, another in Virginia, and lived mostly in a New York City Apartment so I do not know the exact ownership of the comfortable, non-pretentious house we visited, but Kate seemed very much "At Home" there.

Unlike some of our other lunch dates, Kate Smith did not cook

43

lunch—she "ordered out." Pizza and salads for all. As Arlene and Kate ate and talked our camera was rolling:

Born Kathryn Elizabeth Smith, May 1, 1909, in Greenville, Va., she told us, she grew up in Washington, D.C. where her father, William Smith, was a wholesale magazine distributor. She told us she apparently didn't begin to talk until she was about 4 years old but within a year she was singing in church socials and by the time she was 8 she was singing for the troops at Army camps in the Washington area during World War I.

Her father did not approve of her singing activities and made her take up nursing at George Washington University Hospital. She tried nursing for a few months but then quit and got herself a job as a singer on the bill at Keith's Theater. Heading that bill was Eddie Dowling, a well-established headliner and producer. Dowling was impressed by her singing and singed her for a review he was prepping called "Honeymoon Lane." The review opened in Atlantic City, New Jersey, in August, 1926 and moved to Broadway a month later.

Following "Honeymoon Lane," Kate appeared in several other musicals and one evening, Ted Collins, a representative for Columbia Records, saw her and sent a note backstage asking her to see him in his office. When she went to see him a few days later, it turned out to be the beginning of their show-business association. Collins became her manager and put her on the radio in 1931. Her relationship Ted Collins had lasted ever since.

So, lunch over, filming completed, the crew began to pack up and Kate said she had to call a car because she must get back to New York. "Phil and I are going back to New York," Arlene told her. "Would you like to ride with us?" Kate said that would be wonderful.

During the hour or two drive I got to know Kate Smith as the very real, unpretentious person her public image presented to the world. I very well remember when we dropped her off, in front of the New York apartment building in which she lived, she put her hand on my shoulder and said, "Phil. I can't thank you enough for the ride, and you are a great driver."

In the last couple of years I have been hosting a local (Monterey Peninsula) TV Show. I have used Kate's recording of "God Bless America" as the closing theme for each broadcast. If you have not listened to that recording recently or, perhaps, have never listened to it, you should. Kate had a marvelous voice and Irving Berlin's song has never had more meaning than it has today. I have no idea where our country is headed and I doubt I will live long enough to find out. I can only hope for the best.

God, Please Bless America!

The Hotel Dauphin

AS I WROTE EARLIER, the Dauphin Hotel, located on the west side of Broadway between 66th Street and 67th Street, was home to HOME's production staff. Because I spent much, if not most, of my time "on the road" I was not closely involved with many of the staff members but I made a few good friends. One of whom was A,C. Spectorsky.

"Spec" and I shared an office. He was perhaps the most cultured man I ever met. A wonderful gentleman with a droll sense of humor, he was a fine writer and editor and one of HOME's producers. While he was with HOME he published what was perhaps his best known book, "The Exurbanites." He left the show in July, 1956 to join Playboy Magazine, the periodical then best known for its nude centerfolds. Playboy owner, Hugh Hefner, had decided that in order to attract readership by top businessmen and executives, in addition to beautiful nudes, the magazine should also provide intellectual and commercial stimulation. To accomplish this Hefner hired A.C. Spectorsky as literary editor. Spec soon rose to be executive editor and publisher. It is my understanding that Playboy's circulation was something slightly over half a million when Spec joined. Before his untimely death in 1972 (he was only sixty-two years old) the circulation had climbed to over six million.

A story he once told me comes to mind.

Spec and one or two friends loved to go off on fishing trips. For many years they had a guide who took them deep into the back woods where trout were plentiful. The only problem they had with their guide was that he did all the cooking. The tough, heavy pancakes he made for breakfast every morning were almost more than Speck and his friends could eat. So, on their last trip they took with them the makings for crepes suzettes. First morning out they insisted the guide let Spec prepare breakfast and, as he told it, he outdid himself. The crepes were light, wonderful, melt in the mouth delicious. Speck and his friends enjoyed the delightful breakfast. Their guide did not.

"If you're going to have this kind of crap for breakfast," he told them, "I'm quitting!"

He said he needed a breakfast that would stick with him for a long morning of paddling and fishing.

So they went back to heavy duty pan cakes.

Another HOME pal was Al Morgan. At least he was until I perhaps overdid trying to be clever.

Al was another writer/producer for HOME. We did not share an office but we worked together, we palled around some and became friends. Like A. C. Spectorsky, while working on HOME Al was also writing a book, "The Great Man," which was published in 1955. The book quickly became a best seller. Hollywood bought the movie rights and Al left HOME to go to Hollywood to work on the script with Jose Ferrer who was the producer and star.

Hollywood was exciting, wonderful fun and maybe just a little intimidating for Al. He wrote several letters to those of us still working away at HOME, letters that were filled with news about the people he was meeting and the parties he was attending. He wrote of Jose and Julie (London—Ferrer's co-star) of Greg and Betty and Linda and Clark. His letters were filled with the names of famous stars and directors and producers. In a word, Al had become a "name dropper." Sooo, I decided to build a Name Dropper's Kit for him. I typed out the name of every Hollywood personality I could think of, cut each name into an individual slip of paper then put them all in a small box. I then typed out

"Instructions for Use:"

*When looking for a name to drop
reach into this box, pull one out and drop it.
To make a real hit Open the Box,
turn it upside down and have a shower of names.*

I sent the box to him. I never again heard from Al.

I'm sorry Al, it was meant in fun.

My First Pass Port

ABOUT THE SAME TIME Al Morgan and Spec left HOME a new producer named Ted Rogers came on board. He and I became close friends and worked together many times in the years that followed.

One morning, not long after he joined HOME, Ted asked me if I had a Pass Port. No, I did not. "Better get one then," he told me, "I think we are going to send you and Arlene to Japan."

Now isn't that a way to start your day!?

Japan Airlines, JAL, was about to inaugurate direct flight service between Japan and the United States: San Francisco to Tokyo. Seeking ways to promote travel to our former enemy, JAL approached NBC and HOME with a proposal to fly Arlene to Tokyo on the inaugural flight and film her as she visited their country. NBC and HOME agreed on the condition that HOME's Film Director, me, and HOME's Public Relation Director, Elizabeth "Bets" Hagland, accompany her. (NBC was not about to send a female Star out of the country by herself, nor with a young married man without a proper chaperone, consequently Bets was always our companion on foreign locations.)

My first Pass Port was dated December 5th, 1955. My 7th renewal will be due before long, I hope I will have a need for it.

I had always made it a rule to never be away from my family on Christmas. The trip to Japan came close to forcing me to break that rule but fortunately the Inaugural Flight was scheduled to leave San Francisco on December 27th. Consequently Arlene did the show on Monday, December 26th, told her viewers she was going to Japan and would be away until "Next Year" when she would return with lots of wonderful things to "show and tell." And we were on our way.

Immediately after the program Arlene, Bets Hagland and I traveled to Idyllwild Airport (now JFK) and boarded a flight to San Francisco. We spent the night at the Mark Hopkins Hotel high atop Nob Hill then on Tuesday, the 27th, with escorts hovering and cameras flashing, we made our way onto JAL's brand new DC-8 for the late afternoon departure of the long flight that would take us to a world we knew little of.

HOME SHOW STAR—Miss Arlene Francis, with film supervisor and writer Phillips Wylly, waves an enthusiastic farewell to fans of the NBC television show at San Francisco before flying JAL to Japan to film home customs there.

Non Stop flights to far away destinations like Japan were not possible in those long ago days.

Our first stop was Honolulu, Hawaii where we had a four hour layover. We were met at the airport by NBC's local rep and taken to the Royal Hawaiian Hotel for a leisurely dinner then departed Hawaii at 11PM for an all-night flight that took us across the International Date Line to Wake Island where it was early Friday morning, December 29th. Breakfast was served in a military Quonset Hut—a reminder of the so recently ended war. Following breakfast we had an hour or so to walk around and stretch our legs.

The airfield was located right on the ocean front so Arlene, Bets and I walked along the gravel beach. Wake Island looked to be a lonely place and Bets wondered what our GI's on duty there did to entertain themselves. I looked down at the small stones we were walking on and suggested: "They probably marched down here and had a sergeant order them to, 'Count Stones, COUNT!'"

A mid-morning take off from Wake Island put us into Tokyo's Haneda Airport by early afternoon and the beginning of a truly remarkable week.

As we exited the aircraft we were greeted, warmly greeted, by JAL's PR Chief. Tony Senza. (Tony's Japanese name was obviously Anglicized—I remember he told us the Japanese pronunciation which none of us could come close to, maybe Arlene could, I'm not sure.) Fortunately Tony spoke almost perfect English. Along with him was a film crew and half a dozen still photographers. The film crew, Tony told me, was ours to command. They would be with us where ever we went and film whatever we wanted them to film. Tony helped us quickly clear customs then, with film crew following, escorted us to a waiting limousine. He told us he knew we were tired from our long trip and thought we would like time to check in and perhaps rest a bit but he would like to be our host at dinner that evening. Other than that he had nothing scheduled for us until lunch tomorrow when we would be the guests of JAL's President and members of his staff. Following that he had a list of things he thought we might like to see and do. It was indeed a long list.

Our introduction to Tokyo began with the ride to our hotel. Tokyo's streets were wide and jammed full of drivers who paid no attention to any speed limit and had absolutely no idea on which side of the road to drive. I think my first gray hairs sprung out during that ride.

Diner that night began our introduction to Japanese cooking. Realizing few Americans knew much about Japanese cuisine Host Tony carefully guided us through the menu. He suggested we start with a traditional dish, Miso Soup, and gave us a brief description of the ingredients which included various fish and seaweed. Brave visitors that we were, we agreed to "try it." What a surprise, it was delicious!

For a main course Tony recommended Sukiyaki made with Kobe Beef.

Kobe Beef, Tony assured us, was exclusively Japanese. A breed of beef cattle that were hand massaged to produce wonderful, tender, marbleized meat. And to embellish everything we must try Japan's traditional wine, Sake, served hot. Hot wine? They must be kidding, I thought to myself, but we were game for anything so we gave it a try. Today these dishes are well known to all but for us, in long ago 1955, they were experiments in dining that turned out to be truly wonderful. Since then I have eaten Sukiyaki many times, in many parts of the world, but I have never found it to be even remotely comparable to that served in Japan.

Sake, however is a different kettle of fish. Sake, hot Sake, is wonderful where ever you find it!

The following day we were treated to a welcoming luncheon hosted by the President of Japan Air Line. It was there we were first introduced to Sushi.

My mind has a way of recalling some rather minor events while more or less forgetting many far more important happenings. For example, to this day I have a vivid memory of a scene from a war time movie:

Several survivors in a life boat, maybe their ship had been sunk by a submarine, maybe it was their plane that had been shot down, I don't remember that. Nor do I remember the name of the movie or who the stars were. What I did remember—and still do remember—is the scene in which these survivors, far out on the ocean, have reached a point of near starvation when somehow they catch a fish. There is no way they can cook it, so they eat it raw. Nothing could be worse than that, could it? I didn't think so then, I still not sure.

In the face of that memory I was introduced to Sushi. Good lord, its raw fish! Arlene loved it. Bets and I did our best to be good guests.

With our camera crew always at hand, and Tony Senza as our guide, our look at life in Japan began Monday morning with a visit to what Tony assured us was a "typical" Japanese home. We were charmed by the simplicity of the house, its sliding bamboo doors, its furnishings, the small yard that surrounded it and the lovely lady who lived there. She spoke no English but with Tony as interpreter she guided Arlene and our film crew around her home. In the dining room, with its low table and cushions, there was one single item of decoration, a tea cup. An exquisite tea cup with soft colors making a pattern of sorts. As she showed the cup to Arlene she spoke at length about how each day she would look at the cup, hold it in a different light and find peace and tranquility in its beauty. When we returned to New York Arlene spent half a program talking about the simple beauty of that house and that tee cup, and how its owner found new beauty in it, and drew inspiration from it each day.

Next morning we traveled by train to Kyoto. The trip was not long but afforded us a wonderful opportunity to view some beautiful Japanese country side as we sped along. (Even in those distant days Japan boasted hi-speed railroad.) Kyoto is the birthplace of Kabuki. A classical Japanese dance drama that dates back to 1600, Tony told us. It is a stylized dance and music drama with elaborate costumes and make-up and all female rolls are played my men.

That afternoon we were treated to a performance at the Kabuki Theater. Although we did not understand a word of the dialogue, the music, the dance movements and the actor's expressions made clear the story being told. Following the performance we were escorted backstage for a visit with the cast.

Kabuki was a fascinating experience, one I will remember for a long time. Come to think of it, it was an experience I have already remembered for a long time, a very long time! I am not aware of Kabuki being introduced here in America—perhaps it has been, if so it did not have mass appeal. Perhaps seeing it in a Chicago theater might not be the same as in that beautiful theater in far off Kyoto.

Next day another train ride, through more beautiful country. Our destination, Osaka—Japan's third largest city and the birthplace of "Bunraku," Japan's Puppet Theater. If you are like me, or like I was, "puppet" means a small hand held figure, usually somewhat comical in appearance. Not so in Japan's Puppet Theater. Bunraku also dates back to 1600 and is adult drama portrayed by puppets that are between half and three-quarter human size. Each puppet is manipulated by three puppeteers who appear on stage in full view of the audience but clothed in black robes. The main puppeteer controls the face, head, eyes, mouth and right arm of the puppet, number two man deals with the body and left arm, number three handles the lower body and legs. Within about ten seconds of the first puppet's appearance on stage I think Arlene, Bets and I completely forget the puppeteers and were totally mesmerized by the performance of the puppets. As with Kabuki, we had no understanding of the words being mouthed by the puppets (actual dialogue being performed by actors back stage) but their facial expressions and body movements left little doubt as to the story being told. It was almost as if we were watching live Kabuki performed by half size people.

Again, following the performance, we were treated to a back stage visit with "the cast." I had a chance to try my hand at manipulating a puppet's face. The slightest touch on one of the countless little levers located up and down the puppet's "spine" could cause an eyebrow to lift, a mouth to smile, a head to turn or nod or cock to one side. The idea of putting all that together while moving the lips in sync with dialogue from off stage voices was overwhelming. I knew it took years of practice for a devoted artist to master.

All too soon our visit to Japan came to an end. The damn date line thing confused me then and still does today. I believe we left Tokyo on Friday but my pass port indicates we arrived in Hawaii on Thursday, January 5th. I guess that's right—Japan is a day ahead of us??? My mind was so full of things we saw and did it is a wonder I have any memory of leaving. But memories are for sharing and believing in the old adage, "save the best for last," I will wind up this chapter with the story of our New Year's Eve in Tokyo.

Arlene, Bets and I were invited to a New Year's Eve party at our hotel—The Grand Hotel. My faulty memory tells me the party was in some way connected to the American Embassy—virtually all the guests were Embassy people including our Ambassador and his wife—my not so faulty memory tells me it was a rather dull party but some one that evening told us about a beautiful Shinto Shrine located only a short distance from the hotel and of the New Year's ceremony being held there. Visitors were welcome, we decided to have a look.

We were three of hundreds of people making their way down the wide, softly lit pathway leading to the Shrine. On each side of the path, standing proudly at attention, were dozens of uniformed Japanese veterans, some with legs missing, some with arms missing, some blind, all suffering from the catastrophe we remember as World War Two. I thought then as I think now, why do we have wars? Those men standing alongside that path—now becoming our friends—were they any different from the American GI's suffering from the same horrific injuries? How do we let ourselves be dragged into these wars that seem always to be with us? There must be a better way to resolve disputes. A better way to achieve what Wendell Willkey dreamed of: "One World."

(For those of you to whom the name Wendell Willkey is unfamiliar, he was the 1944 Republican candidate for President of the United States.)

KLM–Royal Dutch Airlines

LIFE BECAME even more exciting after I got my pass port; I became a world traveler.

Sunday, the 8th of April, 1956 found me seated next to a very pretty young woman on board a KLM DC-6 en route to Amsterdam. My attractive companion was KLM Airlines Public Relations Director, Betty Nolan. Grace Kelly was to be married in Monaco on the 19th of that month and that was an event made for HOME, but why were Betty and I flying to Amsterdam?

It seems the results of the publicity we generated for JAL were such that somebody from HOME contacted KLM and proposed a similar filmed visit to Holland in return for transportation to Monaco. Betty Nolan and her cohorts thought it a great idea so there I was on my way to Holland where Arlene and I would do some filmed sightseeing much like we had done in Japan just a few months earlier. This time the plan was for me, with help from KLM and Betty Nolan, to scope out some things of interest to film when Arlene joined us a few days later.

Our hotel in Amsterdam was the Grand Hotel Krasnapolsky located on Dam Square more or less opposite the Royal Palace. On arrival Betty introduced me to several KLM people, none of whom I remember by name, but my mind is loaded with memories of Amsterdam.

On my first night there a couple of my new KLM acquaintances took me to a club for a drink The name of that club I remember quite well; at least an Anglicized version of the Dutch name. To me it sounded like "Wine and Fucking." This club, located only a block or two from the hotel, was more than two hundred years old. Hundreds of smoking pipes hung from the low ceiling; pipes that belonged to regular customers who took them down when they wished to smoke. The bar, the bar stools the tables and chairs all looked to be as old as the club itself. In short order I was introduced to a game that had been played there forever. The bartender placed a glass on the bar, a small glass, a bit larger than what we know as a "shot glass," and much more delicate. He then very carefully filled the glass to slightly over the brim with Bols, the famous Dutch gin. Now, a contestant, in this case me, would place his hands behind his back then bend over and try to take a sip of the gin without breaking the surface tension causing it to spill over. Success meant your companions would pay for your drinks that evening, failure meant you would pay for theirs. Well hell, you know I won!

When I woke up next morning I looked out my hotel window which had a commanding view of Dam Square and the traffic circle in its center. What I saw is still vividly implanted in my mind. Bicycles! Literally hundreds of them—people going to work. Holland's economy was still recovering from the war and very few people could yet afford an automobile.

Following breakfast that first morning Betty and her associates took me on a mostly walking sightseeing tour of the city. And what a beautiful city it was. Known as the "Venice of the North," Amsterdam has more than 60 miles of beautiful canals, dug in the 17th century, ringing the oldest part of the city. No one seemed to know exactly how many canals there are but I was told there were more than fifteen hundred bridges crossing them. For someone like me who had never before seen a canal their charm and beauty was unique. I knew when Arlene arrived we would certainly film her taking a boat tour on these lovely waterways, viewing the homes and buildings lining the canals and passing under the many tiny bridges—each one slightly different and more intriguing in design.

Buildings lining the canals—private homes in some places, apartments and office buildings in others—were built so close to the edge of many of these canals people had to walk single file on the narrow sidewalks that separated building from canal. I became aware that many, if not most, of these canal side buildings had a pulley device hanging out over the water from a yard arm at the top of the building. The reason? The only way large items, such as furniture, could be delivered was by barge, then lifted by pulley to a window large enough to accommodate it. You wanna buy a new "fridge"? Never mind how big is your kitchen, how big is your window?

Arlene and Bets Hagland arrived three days after me.

Phil Wylly klapt uit de Amerikaanse T.V. keuken

Our filming began with a visit to an indoor, aquatic tulip market. What do I mean by "aquatic tulip"? Tulips that grow in the water? No, no, this market place was located in sort of an indoor harbor along one of the canals. This harbor had dozens of boat slips into which barges brought tulips, dozens of tulips, hundreds of tulips, thousands of tulips to Amsterdam.. The barges were tied up in different sections of the market so buyers could go to the section offering the color or kind of tulips they wanted. You want red tulips, go to section one; white? Section two, etc. etc. As we learned next day when we visited a tulip farm, there are about ten million different kinds of tulips! Okay, maybe more like a couple of hundred different kinds. But that is a lot of tulips.

It was not long after Arlene arrived that she wanted to try on a pair of wooden shoes. I do not know how comfortable they were but to her credit she wore them much of the time. She wore them as we visited a school for River Boat Families.

Much of the food eaten in Holland, as well as coal, oil and many other necessities, comes from mainland Europe and in the those days these necessities were brought to the Netherlands by river barges. Barges that not only carried produce and products but were homes for the families that sailed them. How did these river barge children get an education? Where did they go to school?

In Europe, at that time—don't know about today—along the rivers of commerce there were special schools located a barge day's journey apart. Schools where river barge children could go for part of a day, or several days. Where they received homework which they could study while floating up or down rivers and turn in next day at the next school. The curriculum was exactly the same at each school so the continuity of study was not disrupted. Even in those distant days European education was well ahead of ours here in America. Not only did young children, I'm talking about ten and twelve year olds, not only did they speak two or three languages, they were proficient in math, science and literature.

Prior to Arlene's arrival I had visited several schools. One I remember was a grade school for "less advantaged children." These were youngsters from low income families—children who were not expected to attend college and who's education was designed to help them find jobs in fields not requiring a degree. After touring the school with the principal a third grade teacher asked me if I would speak to her class. Somewhat embarrassed, I said I would be happy to but I did not speak Dutch. "Oh, that's no trouble. All the children speak very good English," she told me. Most of them, I learned, also spoke at least one other foreign language. I cannot help but think there are things we can learn from Europe's school systems.

As I had expected, one of the filming high lights of our visit to Amsterdam was a canal cruise with Arlene seated in the bow of the small boat in which we sailed. Seen from the canals the various little bridges and buildings were even more picturesque than when seen from the roads and walkways alongside.

Earlier I wrote "Amsterdam was a beautiful city" implying it no longer is. That is not quite my meaning. The city, the old buildings, the canals and bridges are still beautiful but on that first visit to Amsterdam I was impressed, almost amazed at its cleanliness. If you dropped food on the sidewalk you would not be afraid to pick it up and eat it. Some thirty years later I returned to that city. Much had changed. The population had skyrocketed—many people from many lands had immigrated to Amsterdam—the streets were disgusting; dog feces' everywhere, garbage on the sidewalks and in the gutter, it was no longer a city in which I cared to walk.

A trip to the famous van Gogh museum, where several hundred of the master's paintings are on display, and visits to a number of landmark buildings pretty much completed our Dutch tour but I must tell you about one site we saw, but did not film—Amsterdam's Red Light District.

Prostitution was perfectly legal in Holland as it is in many European countries. Someone had told us that before we left the country we ought to have a look at the district. So on our way back from dinner one evening we asked our driver to take us on a tour.

For several blocks buildings that looked much like New York Brownstones lined the road. Each building offered a large window looking into a dimly lit room containing a bed and a scantily dressed young woman (some maybe not so young.) Potential customers walked the sidewalks in front of these buildings, looking in the windows, checking the merchandise. If interested the potential customer would use hand signals to make an arrangement.

Our driver stopped while we watched one such transaction.

A negligee wearing girl was seated on her bed. At her side she had a small box of candy—gum drops, chocolates—don't know. As we watched she put a candy into her mouth. A moment later a potential customer looked in at her. He made a gesture of some sort, she gestured back. One or two more signals and the deal was struck. As the man made his way towards the short stairway and front door, the girl started to the window to pull the curtains. Half way there she stopped, went back to the bed, took one more candy and popped it into her mouth before turning back to close the curtain.

Monaco

ON MONDAY, APRIL 16th, Arlene, Bets and I flew from Amsterdam to Nice, then traveled by auto to Monte Carlo to cover Grace Kelly's wedding scheduled for April 19th. The drive from Nice to Monaco, along the Grande Corniche Highway was memorable indeed. I'm not sure there is any drive more beautiful. Mountains tumble down to the shore line and the narrow highway weaves its way along ridges high above the beautiful Mediterranean Sea. Several very narrow bridges and switch back turns make the ride more than a little bit frightening. (It was one of these turns that one day claimed Grace Kelly's life.)

Grace Kelly grew up in Philadelphia Society. Her father, John B. Kelly, Sr., won three Olympic gold medals for sculling before founding a very successful brick contracting company. As a young girl Grace was very much over shadowed by her two older brothers. They were the apples in her father's eye. Like him, they were very athletic, she was not. Her interests were more in art, music and theatre. She loved to act in school plays. As she grew up she thought more and more about a theatrical career which her father was very much opposed to. None the less, she persisted and in time found great success.

Grace Kelly starred in several major movies and won an Academy Award for Best Actress in "The Country Girl." She was at the top of her career when she gave up Hollywood to marry Prince Rainier.

For us, the three days before the wedding were crazy. Reporters from all over the world had descended on Monaco. Many of them staying in the same hotel as Arlene, Bets, our film crew and I were. Together with many of them we went to event after event:

A spectacular concert at Monaco's beautiful concert hall.

A "Gala" in the casino ball room.

Several luncheons and cocktail parties, and one event I especially remember, a reception for the press on Lady Docker's yacht.

Norah Docker was an English Socialite. According to Wikipedia she was what my generation called "a swinger." She married several times, each time to a man financially better off than the previous one. She always wanted (and got) a bigger yacht. The one we visited was only slightly smaller than the Queen Mary.

At the time of the Royal Wedding she was married to Sir Edmund Docker, who was Chairman of Birmingham Small Arms. The lady and her husband loved to entertain and spend money lavishly. The afternoon reception on board her yacht was spectacular!

Some time later reports indicated that much of Lord Docker's wealth was the result of questionable company expenditures and tax write offs. A year or two after the wedding Prince Rainier banned Sir Edmund and his lady from the French Riviera.

Finally, Wedding Day. By wedding day many of us were too tired or hung over to care. Well, that isn't quite true. We were all excited and fascinated by the pomp and splendor, but I think we were all a bit weary too.

Now, about our visit with Grace and the Prince. Well Arlene got an invitation to the church...er, cathedral, but neither Bets nor I did. Along with a dozen or more other film and TV crews, my crew and I set up on an elevated platform outside the church. The elevated platform gave us an unobstructed view of the church entrance and the crowds waiting for the appearance of the Prince and his bride. Following the ceremony, as the church began to empty we were able to get a shot of Arlene making her way down the cathedral steps and through the crowd. Moments later we were able to film the bridal couple climbing into an open limousine for a ride to the castle. That was as close as any of us got to the Royal Couple.

No one we knew was invited to the reception.

About thirty years later I was Associate Producer/UPM for the made for TV movie: "The Grace Kelly Story." Cheryl Ladd played Grace Kelly, Lloyd Bridges, her father and Diane Ladd (no relation to Cheryl) her mother. I even played a small, make that Very Small, roll as Grace Kelly's escort to the Academy Awards.

Diane Ladd and I worked together several times after that and became good friends. For a time we had "2nd homes" around the corner from each other in Sedona, Arizona. .

Believe it or not, somehow, during those hectic days in Monaco, Arlene and I found time for a very special "At HOME With" visit.

Top of the Hill

I DON'T KNOW just what I expected. A more palatial setting? A more impressive house? Was I really expecting anything other than an opportunity to meet one of my childhood heroes? I had read his poems while I was growing up. I was not, and am not, a person who much cares for poetry but his really got to me and as Arlene and I walked to his front door words he had written many years ago were running through my head:

A bunch of the boys were whooping it up in the Malamute saloon;
The kid that handles the music-box was hitting a jag-time tune;
When out of the night, which was fifty below, and into the din and the glare
There stumbled a miner fresh from the creeks, dog-dirty, and loaded for bear.

Robert W. Service

I knocked on the door. I'm sure he was expecting us but perhaps he had not heard us drive up. Just two cars. Arlene and I in the first and our four man film crew in the second. We didn't make much noise. A moment later the door opened and there he was—tall, slender, 82 years young—"the Bard of the Yukon," Robert W. Service.

While our camera crew set up, Mr. Service and his wife showed us around their charming home. I am not one who remembers details about things like furniture and curtains. All I remember about their home is it immediately felt comfortable. The living room did not look like something out of a magazine, it looked like a room where people lived, the kitchen had the look of a place where wonderful meals were prepared, the dining room a place where they were enjoyed. At the rear of the house there was a lovely terrace around which Mrs. Service had planted a variety of flowers; some white roses were coming into bloom. From that terrace one had a commanding view of the royal castle and all of Monaco spread out against a background of the sparkling blue Mediterranean Sea.

Their house was built high on a hilltop and the vine covered hillside behind it was almost steep enough to be considered a cliff. At the bottom of that cliff ran the glistening railroad tracks that, as Mr. Service proudly told us, carried the Orient Express. He made it clear to us that he loved to watch rail road trains. "My God," I thought, he and I were "simpatico!" Since early childhood I have been fascinated by railroad trains. To this day my wife is terrified when we are out driving and see a train. She knows her life is in danger—my attention is no longer on the road, it is on the railroad train.

Camera ready—Mr. Service and Arlene sat down in the comfortable living room and began to talk about his life: He had been born in England, in 1874, but when he was five years old went to Scotland to live with his aunt Jeannie. While there, at age six, he composed his first poem—a dinner table grace:

> *God bless the cakes and bless the jam;*
> *Bless the cheese and the cold boiled ham:*
> *Bless the scones Aunt Jeannie makes,*
> *And save us all from bellyaches.*
> *Amen.*

Robert W. Service

As a young man, Service found a job that took him to Alaska. He told us of his experiences as a young man in the Klondike where he wrote "Songs of a Sourdough," a book of poems that included "The Shooting of Dan McGrew."

Then I ducked my head, and the lights went out,
And two guns blazed in the dark,
And a woman screamed, and the lights went up,
And two men lay stiff and stark.
Pitched on his head, and pumped full of lead,
Was Dangerous Dan McGrew,
While the man from the creeks lay clutched to the breast
Of the lady that's known as Lou.

Robert W. Service

Mr. Service told of his life during World War One. Being too old for military service he became a battle field Stretcher Bearer and Red Cross Driver. He spoke of the brutality he saw, the wounded, the dying and the dead. It was against that background that he wrote many poems published as "Rhymes Of A Red Cross Man."

Where are you going, Young Fellow My Lad,
On this glittering morn of May?"
"I'm going to join the Colours, Dad;
They're looking for men, they say."
"But you're only a boy, Young Fellow My Lad;
You aren't obliged to go."
"I'm seventeen and a quarter, Dad,
And ever so strong, you know."

Robert W. Service

Mr. Service spoke of their home in Monaco—their yard, his wife's rose garden, their view of the rail road trains below and of the joys of being old, retired, and comfortable there together. As they talked Mr. Service occasionally looked at some reminder notes he had typed up on his old Royal Portable Typewriter then glanced at his wife who was seated not far away. I quickly realized she had a copy of the notes and he was checking with her to make sure he had covered the subjects he had listed. When our day with him ended I was bold enough to ask if I might have the copy Mrs. Service had been working from. Most generously he agreed. He hand wrote a little note to me and autographed the pages. Of course I still have them. The type is a bit faded but they are among my treasured possessions.

To. P Wyllly
with pleasant
memories
Robert Hichens

Answers:

(1)

No, this is my virgin apparition ... I am naturally timid
and shrink from publicity I am afraid I am a born bookman.
My library and my garden mean more to me than the crowded
markets of Vanity Fair. Also I am in my 83rd year, and no
longer have any ambition to be a public entertainer. This
is my first appearance on a television screen and will
probably be my last.

(2)

I think that Television is one of the most formodable
forces of Today. Its potentialities are so enormous
they leave one breathless. They will have a tremendous
influence on future history, and every Government
would do well to foster them. Personally, in the old
of my age Television is a joy and a blessing to me.
Not only am I a fan, —I am a fanatic. We have not much
money to support it here. We are poor and the programs
suffer, but even at that I look forward to it all the

day and evening finds my eyes glued to the screen. Those
who run it seem my friends; the photography gives me
sheer delight, and as a technical miracle I never cease to
regard it with wonder. To one like myself, subdued by the
weight of years the home screen in an armchair by the fire
is a godsend.

Phillips Wylly

I think I have three, —Work, Health and Longevity.
I am dedicated to the job of making verse. It is an
all-day job, because in most of my waking moments I am
incubating lines in my head. On my long walks I am
doping out new stuff, and on my return home very often
I have a bit of rhyme in the bag. The making of it
is a constant joy to me, a rapture of which only ...

As to health it has always been an obsession with me.
The open air, physical culture, the science of food
combinations have all contributed to my physical
care of myself. At fifty I wrote a book called
HOW NOT GROW YOUNG and following out its precepts
has done much to conserve me in fitness and well-being.

As to longevity, frankly I hope to go well into the
nineties. I sometimes think I might achieve the hundred
mark, but this is too optimistic. If some ask: Would
you want to? I answer definitely YES. I enjoy living
the more I get acquainted with it. Even just breathing
is to me a positive pleasure. While all the simple joys
of being seem to me to be intensified by time. Many
days I know rapture, many I join hand with joy,
on nearly all know Content.

71

In addition to the copy of his interview notes, he also gave me a copy of a poem he had written in honor of the new Princes. Typed on his old Royal Portable, there were typos and misspells aplenty, but this is how the great artist worked:

TO G. K.

Princeee, wha t magic pen was dipped
     In radiant colours of romance
To write the wonier of your script,
       Your f~iry tale of chance?
lringing us 'jeauty, Art and Grace
qe welcome to this land of ours;
And with our homage take your place
       'kid song and flowers.
Long may yO!tplay your goll, -mpart,

   Not only to en-sky your name,
 But to be throned i~ every heart
      Nith he orthfire fame.
A people we, proui of our Past,
     ?rom modern urGency afar;
 Long have we hoped .vith faith
           steadfast
   To hail witl, ecstasy a star:
Sweet Princess, may our dream come
       true,Our STAR be you.

Have trouble reading it? Me too. I guess someone "proofed" it before it was sent to the royal household

In my mind Robert W. Service was a very happy, most contented man who lived a life many dream of but few can achieve. More than that, I believe he looked forward to and enjoyed each day as he and his wife puttered in their beautiful garden and he anxiously awaited the daily passing of the Orient Express.

As I write this I realize few, if any, readers will be familiar with the works of Robert W. Service—he died in 1958—but for me the day we spent with him was very special. He was, indeed, a childhood hero.

> *It's a long way to Tipperary,*
> *It's a long way to go;*
> *It's a long way to Tipperary,*
> *And the sweetest girl I know.*

Robert W. Service

I Love Paris

ON OUR WAY back to New York from the wedding, Arlene and I spent a day or two in Paris. My memory does not tell me if Bets was with us, she must have been but she did not attend the luncheon Arlene arranged for us to have with Art Buchwald.

I suspect few if anyone today is familiar with the name Art Buchwald, but back in the 1950ies, and for many years thereafter, Art was a well know, highly acclaimed humorist and syndicated columnist for the New York Herald Tribune. He was a very interesting man.

As our country entered World War II, Art wanted to join the Marines. But he was only seventeen, too young to join without parental or legal guardian consent, and his parents did not share Art's desire. Story goes, he bribed a drunk to sign as his legal guardian and without his parents knowledge, joined up. From October 1942, to October 1945, Art served in the U.S. Marine Corps and spent two years in the Pacific Theater. Following his discharge he enrolled at the University of Southern California, on the GI Bill, where he became Managing Editor of the campus magazine "Wampus," Then, in 1948 he left USC, bought a one way ticket to Paris, and eventually got a job there with the Herald Tribune.

Arlene made our reservation at La Tour D'argent which was then and still is one of the outstanding restaurants in the world! And what a restaurant it was! Located on the second or third floor of a building just above the Seine, it had a spectacular view of Notre Dame Cathedral. Beautifully set tables, a cordial Maitre d' to welcome you, delightful waiters anxious to fulfill your every wish, and food I have no words to describe.

Arlene and Art were good friends. Buchwald lived in Paris, Arlene in New York so just how their friendship came about I have no idea. Makes no difference anyway. Art Buchwald was great fun to listen to and talk with. He and Arlene exchanged many stories and I had a wonderful time dining and listening.

End of story? Not quite.

The 1956 Republican National Convention was held in San Francisco's Cow Palace from August 20th to the 23rd. I was one of the many TV people covering the convention. A Press Conference was called for the afternoon of the 20th and as I walked down a long corridor towards the conference room, who should I meet walking towards me, away from the conference room? Art Buchwald. We exchanged "hellos" and I said "you're going the wrong way—the conference is down there."

"I know," Art said. "But they won't let me in—I haven't got a pass."

Believe it or not, a worldwide syndicated columnist for the New York Herald Tribune could not get into a Republican Convention Press Conference.

"I can't believe it!" I told him. "Come with me, I've got all the passes in the world. I'm sure you can be part of my team."

And that is how a future Pulitzer Prize winner got into the first scheduled press conference for the 1956 Republican National Convention. I did not run into Art at the convention after that, nor did I ever meet up with him again, but I have fond memories of a delightful, warm and witty man who's Herald Tribune columns I had enjoyed for many years before I met him, and continued to enjoy for many years thereafter.

My Date With Sophia

BACK IN THE 1950ies Mike Beck was a very successful publicity agent with an office in New York City. Now I know there is a popular musician/singer named Mike Beck in today's world of 2015—different guy. One of the 1950ies Mike Beck's clients was United Artists—a film production company. One day in 1956, late summer I think, Mike contacted our office to ask if HOME would like to do a "behind the scenes" story about making a film in Spain—United Artists would pay for everything

"What picture?" We asked—not that it would have made any difference, HOME would never pass up an opportunity like that.

"Stanley Kramer is filming 'The Pride and the Passion' in Madrid," Mike answered. The stars were Cary Grant, Frank Sinatra, and a very young, very beautiful but unknown Italian actress named Sophia Loren. (Who would go on to win many awards including an Academy Award in 1962 for the film "Two Women.")

Growing up in the slums of Pozzuoli, Italy, during the second World War, Sophia Loren had experienced much sadness during her childhood:

She grew up in poverty. Her father refused to marry her mother and would not support her and baby Sophia.

During an air raid on Puzzuoli, while running to a bomb shelter, she was struck by shrapnel.

Following the war, together with other family members, Sophia's mother opened a small restaurant where she worked as waitress and dish washer.

Then, in 1950, at age 14 she entered a beauty contest and was one of the finalists. More important, she caught the eye of Italian film producer Carlo Ponti. Under his guidance, by 1956 she had appeared in a number of Italian films but was unknown in the U.S. Mike Beck thought an appearance on HOME would be a good way to promote the film and introduce Loren to American audiences.

So off I went to Madrid.

Let me tell you about my United Artists provided TWA Flight to Spain: The plane I flew in was a Lockheed Constellation. TWA was a major airline in those days and the "Connie" was their big airplane. For you youngsters who never heard of a Constellation, courtesy of Wikipedia, let me give you a brief intro:

The **Lockheed Constellation** *("Connie") was a propeller-driven airliner powered by four 18-cylinder radial Wright R-3350 engines. It was built by Lockheed between 1943 and 1958 at its Burbank, California, facility. Distinguished by a triple-tail design and dolphin-shaped fuselage. The Constellation was used as a civilian airliner and as a U.S. military air transport, It was the presidential aircraft for U.S. President Dwight D. Eisenhower.*

What I remember about the "Connies"—which I had a number of opportunities to fly in—was the three tail fins that made the plane instantly recognizable and the fact that when in the air its wings flapped—like a bird. No, not big flaps, just soft, gentle, up and down movements. I don't think I have ever been in any other aircraft with flapping wings. Okay, I had flown in Connies many times but never First Class to Europe before, and in those marvelous days of yesteryear "First Class" was truly first class! The hostesses made you feel like the most important person in the world; the gourmet meals were outstanding, the wines excellent, the cocktails made from only the finest labels.

Sparing none of UA's money, Mike had booked me into super

first class which meant I had a bunk bed for the overnight flight. Yes, an honest to goodness bed much like a lower birth in a rail road Pullman Car. After a wonderful dinner and an after dinner drink my bed was made up by two very attractive TWA Hostesses. (I know what you're thinking but no, First Class treatment did not go that far!)

So, well rested, I arrived in Madrid where I was met by a delightful gentleman named Dick Condon, Richard Condon. The Richard Condon who wrote "The Manchurian Candidate" and a number of other very popular books. But Dick had not started his literary career back then, he was working as a Press Agent for United Artists. With Dick, was a uniformed man I took to be our chauffer. No doubt I should have known better but you see I had not traveled at quite this level before. The man was not our chauffer, he was our footman—that fellow who sits next to the chauffer and does things like open and close limousine doors and, in this case, get luggage.

Outside the airport our chauffer and limousine were waiting.

The word "Limousine" may be a bit misleading. The staffing—chauffer and footman—was perfect, but that designation of the vehicle is stretching it a bit. You see, in 1956 the Spanish economy had not recovered from World War Two. The vehicle was, I think, of 1931 or 1932 vintage. Clean and polished but nearly 25 years old. Old perhaps, but fully capable of comfortably carrying us to the Ritz Hotel. (Just how a hotel in Madrid, Spain came to be named "The Ritz" is beyond me, but it was—and still is—a very fine hotel.) While Dick waited in the lobby two young bell boys escorted me to my room. I was aware the Spanish economy was much different from ours so I was not sure how much to tip the two boys (who were probably not more than twelve or thirteen years old.) I decided on one dollar each. The boys took the money, gave me something of a murmured "thanks" and hurried out of the room. I asked Dick if I had given them too small a tip. He laughed and shook his head telling me "no," the boys probably did not make that much money in a week and at that very moment might well be negotiating to buy the hotel.

That evening, in our "limousine" we went out to dinner. As we drove down the beautiful Paseo del Prado an elegantly dressed older couple drew alongside us. She was wearing a fur stole over a full length gown, he was in a tuxedo complete with top hat. I was able to clearly see their fine attire because they were driving a Vespa. A very tiny motor bike.

Somewhere along the way Dick Condon gave me the news. Filming of "The Pride and the Passion" had been completed. Stanley Kramer, Cary Grant and Frank Sinatra had all returned to the U.S. Sophia Loren had returned to her home in Rome.

"Well gee, Dick, what-a-ya think we should do now?" I asked.

"Got it all planned," Dick answered. "In a couple-a-days we will go to Rome and visit Sophia."

How tough could that be?

So a couple-a-days later, after carousing Madrid's night clubs, restaurants and Flamingo halls, we flew to Rome (First Class of course.) and with film crew in tow arrived one morning at Miss Loren's door

Sophia Loren was apparently living with her mother. Or was her mother living with Sophia? I'm not quite sure which, but the apartment seemed to be occupied by them both, and both welcomed us warmly. It was going to be a delightful visit. Except—I was sick.

Two days of Spanish food and drink had completely destroyed my bowel functions. As this photo of Sophia and myself, and Dick Condon's description indicate, I was so constipated by the time we reached Sophia's home I was actually in pain.

Voted "grea test screen still of all time" by the
citizens of Olliufia,picturesque suburb of Trieste
this scene from "Salami Duro" co-starring America's
idol Phillips Wylly and the Italian bombshell,Sophia
Loren tells a story of passion unashamed. In it
Wylly,playing the heart-breakimg role of the inventor
of the Vespa flings his naked soul headlong down
the stairway of his life the instant he comes up against
Miss Lorán,playing the cruel monopolist who controls
the Milano supply of all the small tires so vital
for the completion of the little scooter. How,in one
still an actor wven of Wylly,'s artistry can register
the fact that he he at once trustrworthy,loyal,helpful,
friendly,courteous,kind,obedient,cheerful,thrifty
clean and reverent,is cause for wonderment,if not awe.
His hair styles are by Hammacher,Schlemmer;his eyes
by Corning Glass.

Richard Condon may be better known for "The Manchurian Candidate" but I have always thought this is his best work!

Shortly after this photo was taken Sophia's mother came to my rescue.

While under Dick's direction, the film crew began filming Sophia, her mother took me into the kitchen and prepared something for me to drink. I have no idea what it was, but it worked. Within a few hours I was functioning properly and feeling better. Not great, but at least okay. Well enough to at least thank Sophia—and her mother—and tell her how anxious I was to see her again when she came to New York to be Arlene's on air guest. Well enough too, to enjoy the dinner Dick Condon had arranged for us that evening.

If you walk down "The Spanish Steps" to the Piazza di Spagna—the street at the bottom of the steps—then turn to the right, a short way down that road, on the left hand side, there was a restaurant. Actually there were a lot of restaurants along that street. I wish I could remember the name of the one I want to tell you about. For all I know it may still be there, I know it was 20 years ago when I revisited it. Anyway, we sat at a table large enough to accommodate us all, Dick, our cinematographer, two or three other crew members and me. (I wish I could report that SHE was with us, but she wasn't.)

As we prepared to order dinner, Dick asked for wine. The waiter quickly produced a huge flagon of red wine. He sat it down on the table, took a crayon from his pocket and carefully drew a line on the flagon at the level of the wine. Several hours later, as we finished our meal and asked for the bill, the waiter again drew a line on the bottle at what was then a much lower level of wine. He then measured the distance between the first line and the second line. Our charge was based on the indicated usage.

There is a short follow up to this story: Almost 50 years later my wife Shirley and I, together with her son Mark, who was living in Switzerland at the time, were vacationing in Rome. One day we found ourselves at the top of the Spanish Steps. It was nearing lunch time. "I know a good place for lunch," I told them, and led them down the steps to Piazza di Spagna and to where I hoped the restaurant in which Dick, the crew and I had dinner would still be. It was. The food was as good as I remembered and Mark was very impressed by the fact that I knew where in Rome a fine Italian Restaurant was located. (No, they no longer priced wine consumption by crayon markings on the bottle, they charged by the glass. But it was not too expensive.)

CUT! PRRR-INT!
and
Joan of Arc

ARLENE AND I met Joan of Arc in Paris one day in early March 1957. Understand there are two "Joans" I am writing about. The first one was burned at the stake by the British in 1431. The second, a young actress named Jean Seberg, was burned at the stake by a British Film Crew just a few days before Arlene and I met with her alongside Emmanuel Fremiet equestrian sculpture, *Jeanne d'Arc,* which is located at the Place des Pyramides in Paris. That location is said to be where the first Joan of Arc was wounded during her failed attempt to take the city. Nicknamed "The Maid of Orleans," Joan of Arc is a folk heroine of France and a Roman Catholic saint. Claiming divine guidance, she led the French army to several victories during the Hundred Years War before she was captured, sold to the British then, in May of 1431, burned at the stake. She was nineteen years old.

Not much older, the second Joan of Arc was a very pretty young lady from the Tall Corn State.

Apparently United Artists and Mike Beck were pleased enough with our story about Sophia Loren to want to try the same introduction for Jean Seberg, another unknown actress from Marshalltown, Iowa. Right, Iowa, where the Tall Corn grows. According to publicity already released Jean Seberg had won a talent search conducted by Producer, Director, Otto Preminger who had tested 18,000 young women for the roll of Joan of Arc in the movie "Saint Joan" he was preparing to produce. 18,000 does seem like a very large number of people to test but as Paul Simon's song says, "Who am I to Blow Against the Wind?"

Regardless of how many young women were or were not tested, Jean Seberg was signed to play the leading roll and UA and Mike thought a TV appearance on HOME would be a good idea. Mike suggested Arlene and I travel to London, where Preminger was filming the picture. Arlene thought a trip to England would be nice and me? Well if I had to go, I had to go.

To London, that is.

Modus Operandi as usual: I preceded Arlen and Bets Haglund by a couple of days, arriving in London, according to my pass port, the evening of Wednesday, February 27, 1957. A studio car awaited my arrival and quickly took me to the Dorchester Hotel where a small suite awaited my arrival. Lovely hotel, the Dorchester. First class in every way!

Thursday morning another studio car took me to the Shepperton Studio and my meeting with "the man."

Shepperton Studio, in the mid-fifties, was a fascinating place. Surrounded by a high wall—stone I think—it had huge wrought iron gates that looked as if they should be tended by lance carrying guards wearing 16th century uniforms. As you passed through the gate you had the feeling you were going back into the England of yesteryear when the sun never set upon the British Empire. Once inside the wall my guide took me to a stage door where the red light was blinking. We waited for a few moments until the light went off then entered to find Joan of Arc tied to a stake and fire being lighted at her feet. I watched as the flames grew, Saint Joan screamed, then Otto Preminger's German accented voice called out loud and clear, "Cut! … Prrrint!"

The flames went out, Jean Seberg was helped down from stake and Otto Preminger came towards me with his hand extended. "Mr. Wylly, how nice to meet you." He quickly introduced me to his "second unit" cameraman who would film anything I wanted, then Otto went back to work.

Joan went back to the stake.

Otto Preminger called for "Action."

And my camera crew began filming set activity.

For those of you who may not be familiar with the words, "Cut," and "Print," let me clue you in. Other than for profanity, these are two of the four most commonly heard words on a motion picture set. The other two being: "Roll," and "Action." In order of usage their definitions are as follows:

Roll—means start the camera.

Action—means actors start acting

Cut—means actors stop acting and camera stop filming

Print—means the performance just filmed was satisfactory and the film just exposed should be sent to the lab for processing

Otto Preminger was more or less at the height of his career in 1957. He had produced and directed a number of top rated films including, "Laura," "Stalag 17," "The Man With The Golden Arm," "Anatomy of a Murder," and "Exodus." "Saint Joan" did not turn out to be one of his best and contest winner Seberg's performance was not high on the critics list, but I am getting ahead of myself. When I met Otto he was a top dog in the film world and his pictures made lots of money.

No matter how comfortable first class accommodations are, airplane rides were not times when I got a lot of sleep so by late Thursday afternoon, when "wrap" was called, I was ready to get back to my hotel and "hit the hay," as we farmers always say. Otto had things to do, he wished me a good night's rest and told me in the morning we could ride together in his car to the studio for what was to be the final day of shooting.

Otto Preminger had a reputation for being something of a ladies man. Friday morning I began to realize just how well deserved that reputation was. Inside the car waiting for me I found Otto and a very attractive young woman who's name I do not remember. Our conversation, as we drove to the studio, made it clear that the young lady and Otto were roommates who fully enjoyed each other's company. Otto was married at the time but the young woman with him was not his wife, where his wife was I have no idea and it was none of my business anyhow.

In time we arrived at the studio. Otto and his companion kissed goodbye and she was off for a day of shopping in preparation for what was to be a "Picture is Wrapped," celebratory weekend. As we waved and watched the studio limo make its way back through the wrought iron gates, Otto told me he was sorry to desert me for the weekend but they had made special plans and he hoped I could find something to do by myself. Actually there was something I wanted to do. Somewhere I had seen a poster announcing Pearl Bailey's appearance at Grosvenor House, an upscale hotel on Park Lane, and I wanted to see her show if I could get a reservation.

Back in my high school days, in Buffalo, New York, I was well on my way to a career in music. The Anchor Bar in Buffalo (yes, where they invented Buffalo Wings) featured a pianist named Dave Rivera who, along with a good tenor sax man and a very good string bassist, made music I loved to hear. Over the course of the six or seven months we lived in Buffalo, Dave and I became friends and about the time we were to move back to Long Island (Dad had found a new job) Dave announced he was leaving Buffalo too. He had landed a job with Cab Calloway. (Cab who? Cab Calloway. He led one of the top swing bands of the thirties and forties.)

A few months later, when we were living back in Port Washington, Cab Calloway's band, along with singing star Sister Rosetta Tharp, opened at the Capitol Theatre in New York. Bob Renfrew (a close friend) and I went to hear/see the show. We got there early and went first to the Stage Door where we sent a message to Dave Rivera. A couple of minutes later Dave popped out and we had a hug and handshakes reunion. "How come you're here?" Dave wanted to know.

"To see you and dig the band and Sister Rosetta." I told him.

"Me and the band you can dig, but not Rosetta," he told us. "She got sick. A new girl is taking her place—Bill Bailey's sister—her name is Pearl, I think."

Ten years later Pearl Bailey was an international star.

Otto was delighted that I had something in mind to do. Getting a reservation would be no problem, he assured me. His secretary secured a ringside table in less time than it took for him to ask her to do so.

A few minutes later, as we passed through the wardrobe department on our way to the set, Otto nodded his head towards a pretty young girl who was doing something with costumes, "That might be something for you…" he told me. "Her name is Tasha." I'm sure I blinked. I may have said something, I have no idea what. Thoughts of pretty girls had not been in my mind but one look at Tasha quickly put them there. Pearl Bailey's show would be great, but it would be more fun to have someone to go with wouldn't it? But would she go with me? I'm a married man with two kids, what was I thinking of?   Frankly, I was thinking of Tasha. It was kind of late to ask a girl for a date on Friday evening but what the heck, I could ask. A couple of drinks, dinner and a show, how bad would that make me? So I asked her. "Mr. Preminger told me if I ask real nice, you might have dinner with me tonight."

She said "yes."

We had ringside seats, a bottle of champagne, and dinner, courtesy of U.A. and my new friend Otto. And Pearl was truly great! After her show I sent one of my business cards back stage with a note telling her of seeing her the day she took over for Sister Rosetta Tharp. In almost no time our waiter returned with word that Miss Bailey would very much like to have us join her in her dressing room. We had fun talking about her big break with Cab Calloway's band and how life had been good to her since then, and before we knew it the stage manager was knocking on the door to let Pearl know it was almost time for her second show. "I hope you'll stay," she told us, and we were delighted to do so.

GROSVENOR HOUSE,
PARK LANE,
LONDON, W. I.

TELEPHONE: GROSVENOR 6363.
TELEGRAMS:
GROVHOWS, AUDLEY, LONDON.

March 14, 1957

Dear Mr. Wiley:

Thank you so much for dropping by to
see me and reviving wonderful memories
of Cab and Sister Thorpe. I still say
I'm sorry she had the sore throat, but
it was certainly the turning point of
my career.

Kindest regards,

Pearl Bailey

PB:dl

I have given a lot of thought about what follows; not just sure what past secrets I should reveal. Finally decided there really is no one left who will be hurt or overly embarrassed so reveal I shall.

Following the second show, as we left Grosvneor House Tasha hugged my arm and told me it was so late she really didn't want to make the long subway ride back to her place and could she stay with me.

And she did.

Early Monday morning Tasha and I kissed goodbye. She headed back to her job at the studio. I headed to the airport to meet Arlene and Bets Haglund.

CUT. PRINT!

I guess some people can sleep on overnight flights; Arlene and Bets among them. Arlene had done her regular "What's My Line" TV show Sunday evening then she and Bets caught a late flight to London and here they were, bright and ready to go. I told them we had a date for cocktails with Otto that afternoon if they felt up to it and they assured me they were. So, that afternoon, over Crystal Champagne and Beluga Caviar in Otto's suite, we made plans to film Arlene and Jean Seberg in Paris.

Tuesday we traveled to France and wonderful accommodations at the George V Hotel. Then, over the next three days, we filmed Arlene and Jean Seberg at the Jeanne d'Arc equestrian sculpture. We filmed them at the Arch D'Triumph (which has nothing to do with Joan of Arc but certainly a lot to do with Paris and France.) and several other well know landmarks. During our evenings we wined and dined at The Lido, the Folies Bergere, one night at the Crazy Horse Saloon and Show Room where it took me several minutes to realize the beautiful young women dancers were not wearing any clothing. What appeared to be costumes was actually shadows created by magical theatrical lighting.

The Crazy Horse was fun, champagne and caviar was wonderful, Seberg in Paris was good—made a nice show segment—getting to know Otto Preminger was a real delight and meeting Pearl Bailey wonderful, but you know what made the trip for me, what I shall never forget? Of course you do—Tasha. I hasten to add "Tasha" is not her real name. Her real name is somewhat exotic as well, but no one really needs to know it.

PS: Two or three weeks after returning from Paris I was sitting at my desk in the Dauphin Hotel when the phone rang. I answered and our receptionist, in a rather awed tone of voice, told me Otto Preminger was on the line. I answered quickly, we exchanged "hellos," then he told me he was setting up an office in New York and did I know any girls. Now I have to tell you, Otto's call was a complete surprise, his question mind boggling. Other than sudden thoughts of Tasha, I'm not sure just what was running through it. I think I said something like, "Are you looking for an office girl or a girl?" I think he indicated he needed a secretary type. I think I told him I didn't have anyone in mind but would check the people in our office. I don't think I ever got back to him and I don't know if anyone in our office did either.

Cut. Print. Wrap.

There Was No Place Like HOME

HOME WENT OFF the air in July of 1957. Julian Goodman had replaced Pat Weaver as NBC's President and the new administration decided to make massive changes in NBC programming. I am not at all certain of my facts but many programs were canceled and some 2,000 people reportedly laid off. Home was one of the canceled shows and, two months short of my ten year pin, I was one of two thousand.

Julian Goodman was the man who brought Johnny Carson to the Tonight Show. Gosh Julian, Johnny lasted for 30 years. How come I was only good for ten? (Probably just as well he isn't around to answer that question.)

One of the few regrets I have with respect to HOME is the fact that I never got to know Hugh Downs very well. When Arlene and I traveled the world, Hugh stayed at HOME. I can think of only one time when my film crew and I worked with Hugh. He was a delightful man who went on to many important projects with NBC. I wish I could have spent more time with him.

But working with Arlene Francis was the opportunity of a lifetime. She was amazing. Her mind was incredible and she always did her "homework." We would go off to interview people and she never had notes to look at. It was all in her mind. And her memory was unbelievable. I recall once being at a reception held for her at an NBC Affiliate somewhere in the Midwest. Standing in the reception line, she was introduced to fifty or more people. All important to NBC. As cocktails were served Arlen wandered about the room chatting with as many of the guests as possible. She would ask where they came from and, because during her film career she had made personal appearances in almost every place you can think of, invariably she would have some memory about whatever city it was. "Is there still that wonderful candy store on Main Street?" she would ask. "Does the high school football team still wear red and white?" "Is Frank Smith still the manager of the RKO Theater there?"

How she could do that is far beyond me. But she could. And she did. No guest left that party without the belief the Arlene Francis was a very special person. Indeed she was.

And Arlene was truly a pioneer. As far as I know she was the first woman to "host" a one hour a day (Monday through Friday) network television program. Barbara Walters, Oprah Winfrey, and Ellen DeGeneres, all, I think, owe a small debt of gratitude to Arlene. She broke the ice…or was it a Glass Ceiling?

Knowing and working with Arlene Francis has to rate very high in the list of wonderful things that have happened to me. How could I have been so lucky?

The Future Begins Now

For me the next six years were difficult, challenging and in many ways rewarding. I had never before been unemployed. I had a wife and two children to support. How? Where? Doing what? The first answer came from Ted Rogers. Ted, who had been HOME's last producer, had become a producer for NBC's Sunday afternoon program: "Wide Wide World." Not long after HOME's demise Ted offered me an assignment to put together and direct a WWW segment dealing with the FBI training base at Quantico, Virginia. The project was something of a coup for Wide Wide World because the FBI base had been pretty much "hush, hush" before; off limits to reporters, inquisitive people and groups. A coup for NBC, a very big coup for me. I believe the unit I took to Quantico was the first non-government TV Crew ever allowed on the base. It was a great experience. I met several "G-Men" who became casual friends and received a very nice note from "The Man" himself, J. Edgar Hoover.

OFFICE OF THE DIRECTOR

UNITED STATES DEPARTMENT OF JUSTICE
FEDERAL BUREAU OF INVESTIGATION

WASHINGTON 25, D. C.

December 23, 1957

PERSONAL

Mr. Phillips Wylly
Wide Wide World
National Broadcasting Company
30 Rockefeller Plaza
New York 20, New York

Dear Mr. Wylly:

I wanted to drop you this personal note in order to commend you for the excellence of your direction of the portions of yesterday's Wide Wide World television program which were on film. The segment of the program dealing with the FBI was exceptionally well done, and your contributions were certainly significant.

Sincerely yours,

The World of Advertising

SHORTLY AFTER MY VENTURE into the world of the FBI, Ted called to tell me his friends at Compton Advertising were looking for a Commercial Producer and suggested I contact them. It seemed as though my life with NBC was over.

The 1950ies were good years for film makers in the world of advertising. The use of filmed commercials had been increasing year after year and had been given a real shot in the arm in 1949 by none other than one of the all-time baseball greats: All Star, Hall of Famer, only pitcher ever to have scored 36 victories in one season, Dizzy Dean. Dean helped the St. Louis Cardinals become League Champions and World Series Champions several times during the 30ies and 40ies. When his pitching career was cut short by a freak accident he turned his talents to broadcasting where his country boy style of speaking made him a popular TV sports personality.

So, come the 1949 World Series Dean was doing "color" commentary and "live" commercials from the TV booth in Yankee Stadium. One of his sponsors was a well know tire manufacturer. The big item they were promoting that year was a self-sealing tire which, if punctured, would not deflate. The commercial Dizzy was to do called for him to drive a large nail into one of those fully inflated, indestructible tires as he extolled its virtues in the wonderful, country style language Dizzy was known for.

"This here now tire," Dizzy told his viewers as he placed a large nail on the tire he clutched between his knees and lifted a hammer. "This here tire is juss what-chu want when you take your family for a ride." With that, Dizzy brought the hammer down and drove the spike into the tire. The loud "pop" and a louder hiss that followed almost drowned out Dizzy's "OH SHIT!"

From that day forward most "demonstration" TV commercials were filmed. (Or in today's world, Video Taped.)

I owe a debt of gratitude to Dizzy Dean because the increasing use of filmed commercials is probably what opened Compton's door for me. I was hired to produce commercials for Personal Size Ivory Soap, (Proctor and Gamble was Compton's biggest client) Comet Cleanser, and Rheingold Beer. Three things I remember about Compton Advertising:

First, the Rheingold Beer song:

> *My beer is Rheingold the dry beer,*
> *Think of Rheingold whenever you buy beer,*
> *It's not bitter, not sweet,*
> *Just a dry flavored treat*
> *Won't you try won't you buy*
> *Rheingold Beer.*

Second, an account executive named Vera who proclaimed the greatest word in the advertising lexicon is "NEW!" Thus, while I was with Compton, Personal Size Ivory became "NEW Personal Size Ivory" and Comet Cleanser became "NEW Comet Cleanser." As far as I know there were no actual changes in the products. (But, I assure you, no Comet Cleansed sink was ever seen unclean no matter how many "takes" it took!)

Third, and certainly the best thing that happened to me while working at Compton, was meeting a fellow commercial producer named Bill Wilson. More about Bill later.

A quick side note: Motion Picture commercials, movies, "Sit Coms" and dramatic shows were, and still are, enormously popular. Popular not only in the non-cable world of old but everywhere. Charlie and Albert and Leonard had been right, film companies did take over much of TV. Unfortunately for them newsreel production was not a part of that and within five years after my leaving RKO Pathe, all five major newsreel companies had gone out of business.

In spite of the obviously expanding business at Compton, and the opportunities that might result, producing commercials was not really my cup of tea. All those exciting years at NBC left me itchy for more action, more travel, more people to meet. As a result, next time Ted Rogers telephoned I was more than anxious to learn what he wanted.

Hollywood at Last

ASSOCIATED TELEVISION, better known as ATV, was one of the first private TV Networks allowed in Great Brittan. ATV was owned by Lew and Leslie Grade and the story I heard was that because the company was making so much money in still economically stressed England there was talk in Commons about taking away its license. Then the Grade's had a brilliant idea, they would become active in the US, sell British made programs there and bring much needed money into Great Brittan. Result? Government blessing, and the Grade's went looking for the best way to do that. What they really wanted was an American partner.

About that same time a Texas oil millionaire named Jack Wrather was looking for a way to take his production company international.

When Jack Wrather was a young man he left Texas for Hollywood where he married movie star Bonita Granville and, with plenty of money, bought the rights to a number of TV shows: The Lone Ranger, Lassie and The Gale Pitts Show among them. Jack's desire was to make The Wrather Corporation into an international presence and the Grade's seeking an American partner made for a match that was perhaps not made in heaven but, late in 1958, did result in the formation of ITC, International Television Corporation. Not too long after that, Wrather hired Ted Rogers to head up ITC. Ted's call to me in early February, 1959, was to ask if I would like to come to Hollywood and join him at ITC. Need I tell you I jumped at the idea.

Talk about being a "lucky man"—my wife, Ruth, was all for the idea. Never mind the fact that we had just had our third son—he was born on Thanksgiving Day, 1958. Never mind the fact that our two older boys were in school and it would mean leaving her and the kids in Port Washington until the school term ended while I went quickly to LA. Damn the torpedoes, straight ahead! Off I went. Ruth sold our house in Port Washington then she and the boys joined me in early June. Soon we bought a house in Tarzana and all was right with the world. For a while.

The marriage of ATV and Wrather Productions proved to not be a happy one. Jack Wrather wanted to produce new programming, ATV wanted to sell British programming in the US. Eventually ATV bought out Wrather's interest. Ted left the company and for a while I became head of production for a company that really did not want to produce in the US. None the less we had one series pilot, "Frontier Correspondent," at CBS and the word seemed to be "GO!" I'm not certain about all the details but CBS apparently bought the show and had it scheduled for the fall lineup. We were about to go into production when CBS called and told us "STOP."

The deal was off.

I know a cancellation like that must have cost CBS some money, but they did not seem to care. Story I heard later was this: Jack Benny had a production company and his company had also produced a series pilot. It was apparently between Benny's pilot and ours for which one got the time slot. CBS had decided on us. Shortly after Jack's agents received the news they advised CBS that Jack Benny had decided not to return to CBS next fall. He was so discouraged about his pilot, and getting a bit tired of the regular Sunday Night Show that he had decided to retire from TV.

I imagine that bomb shell shook up everybody at CBS. The thought of losing their number one Sunday night program was devastating. So, quick as a wink, they dumped us and bought Benny's program.

Then the ITC production arm was closed down and I was devastated.

Being out of work and virtually unknown in Hollywood was not a happy time for the Wylly's. It was then that NBC called again.

New York, Back Again

REMEMBER MY MENTION of Bill Wilson, a commercial producer at Compton Advertising? Not long after ITC Production closed down I got a call from Bill. Seems he had made a deal with NBC Television to produce two, hour long documentaries. One was to be titled "Debutante '62" the second, "The Vanishing 400" based on Cleveland Amory's book, "Who Killed Society?" Bill called to ask if I would care to return to New York and join him as his Associate Producer. Indeed I would!

By the time Bill's call came we Wyllys were living on a shoe string. The job at NBC would not start for five weeks. We had enough money to fly the family back to New York. We could stay with Ruth's mother and sister until new income would allow us to rent a house. But spending a month living at Ruth's mother's house did not appeal greatly to either Ruth or me. We decided we had enough money and plenty of time to drive slowly across the country, camping out in all sorts of wonderful places. So we did. Yosemite, The Grand Teatons, Yellowstone. We camped where Custer made his Last Stand, we camped at Mt. Rushmore and wondered at the faces of George Washington, Thomas Jefferson, Abraham Lincoln and Theodore Roosevelt looking down at us.

We fished, we hiked, we had a month none of us will ever forget.

Then, New York.

How Bill Wilson got to NBC and the "you would never guess" connection between Bill and Ted Rogers is a story I wish I knew more about, but what I do know is well worth telling:

Sometime after I left Compton Advertising, Bill left to become TV Guru for the John F. Kennedy presidential campaign.

Not long after Ted's job at ITC ended he became the TV Guru for Richard Nixon's presidential campaign.

You know which candidate won and you may remember it was generally conceded it was their TV appearances that swayed the vote. Result: Bill Wilson could write his own ticket. Ted Rogers was looking for work.

The two, hour long documentaries I did with Bill were modestly successful.

"Debutant '62" was the first to go into production.

The basic idea for "Debutant '62" was for our cameras to visit one, two, or more debutant balls and get to know some of the young women involved. Bill had engaged a director who had a good Hollywood reputation. His name is unimportant. Directing a movie with a script and rehearsal time was his cup of tea; the problem was, grabbing shots during a real happening and following someone about as they did what they had to do was not. That is what I had done for four years on "HOME." So pretty quickly I took over the directing job.

Finding Debutant Parties willing to have us invade their inner sanctum was not an easy task. One spectacular party Bill had heard about was to be in Dallas, Texas. But how to set it up? Bingo! I knew how. Or I thought I did.

As mentioned before, Jack Wrather was from an old Texas millionaire family. So were most of his executives. One in particular, J.T. Price, had been a great friend of Jack's father and of most of the oil wealthy Texans in Dallas. He had also become a good friend of mine while I was with ITC. So, I telephoned him.

"I'll take care of it," J.T. told me.

And he did. The lovely young lady who would became Dallas' Debutant of that year was our star. We filmed her and her family, we filmed her at school, we filmed her shopping and prepping for the ball, we filmed the ball itself.

We also covered the Black Debutant ball in New York City. My first interview with the woman who was basically in charge of the event got off to a slow start. I think she was not entirely comfortable with the idea of a white film crew invading their event. Talk about luck, that day was a very lucky one for me. As she and I were talking a gentleman came into the office. I did not know him but he looked familiar. She introduced us. . His name I knew very well. He was an orchestra leader and he and his band were going to play for the ball. Believe it or not, Dave Rivera had once told me about maybe going to work for him. I told him hello, told him I had a couple of his records and asked him if he was still in touch with Dave.

You could almost hear the ice breaking.

Ten minutes later, after mostly talking about music (did I ever tell you I started out wanting to be a musician?) "Debutant '62" was welcomed to cover the ball.

Everyone was happy with "Debutant '62" and, as a result, Bill asked me to direct our second project, "Who Killed Society."

"The Vanishing 400" author Cleveland Amory helped with our "Who Killed Society" script and acted as an associate producer. Consequently I got to know "Clip" slightly. He was born into a socially prominent Boston family in 1917. He went to Harvard and was President of the "Harvard Crimson." After graduation he became the youngest editor ever of "The Saturday Evening Post." He became a "social historian," satirist and critic. He wrote a number of books, and was an on-air editor for the TODAY show.

But Clip's real passion was animal rights. He could talk forever about the cruelty inflicted on animals and had traveled the world leading causes against the senseless killing of animals. At one time he ran a crusade against fur coats and got a number of Hollywood stars to participate. The executive director of the Humane Society of the United States once described Amory as "the founding father of the modern animal protection movement."

We were delighted to have Walter Pidgeon as Host and Narrator for "Who Killed Society" Pidgeon was best known for his role in the Academy Award nominated film, "Mrs. Miniver," for which he received a Best Actor nomination. He did not win but his co-star, Greer Garson, won Best Actress for her performance in the title role. Walter and I worked together for only a few days. He was a warm, friendly and considerate man.

Working with Walter Pidgeon and getting to know Cleveland Amory even casually was great. Our show? Well it got some nice write ups and NBC seemed happy.

We had no more than "wrapped" Society, when I got a call from Reuven Frank.

Telstar

BACK WHEN Paul Alley's NBC TV Newsreel became The Camel News Caravan, and Paul was suddenly looking for work, Reuven Frank was one of the first writers hired for the new show. We became friends. In the years since then Reuven had climbed the NBC ladder to become a senior producer and was starting work on a major project, "Telstar," the name given to a three country project to present the first, international, live TV telecast..

Here in the year of 2015 there are not too many people familiar with the 1962 brand of television. In 2015, as we watch our TV News switch from the central studio in New York to a reporter in London, then to a reporter in Afghanistan, then another in Hong Kong, it is hard to realize that in 1962, at least the first half of 1962, the only TV from outside the country was on film or video tape delivered by air... not through the air but by air planes. Then came Telstar.

Telstar was the first communication satellite. It was the product of a multi-national agreement between AT&T, Bell Telephone and NASA; GPO, Great Brittan; and National PIT, France. Telstar One was launched on top of a Thor Delta rocket on July 10th, 1962. It successfully relayed through space the first television pictures and provided the first transatlantic television feed.

Preparations for that first transatlantic TV began many months before the rocket's launch. Unbelievably large and complex antennas were being constructed in rather out of the way locations in each of the three participating countries. The US antenna, near Andover, Maine. The British installation at

Goonhilly Downs, near Lands End. The French antenna at Perros-Guirec on the English Channel. Reuven wanted film of the three installations and hired me to get it for him. So, in April, 1962, along with writer John Apple, (who later became a well-known correspondent for the New York Times), Production Manager Al Vechione, and, first, a film crew from NBC New York, then a crew from BBC London, I was off to see and film the world of Telstar.

And an amazing world it was!

In the Maine woods, not far from Andover, we found a large area that had been cleared and therein was built a small village: motel like housing, a kitchen and dining hall, a medical office, a small shop where one could buy various personal items such as tooth paste, cigarettes, snack food, etc. etc. and a huge, inflated plastic tent, covering an area more than two hundred feet by two hundred feet, in which a giant, megaphone shaped antenna road on a circular rail. While the antenna rotated on the rail, the "megaphone" rose up and down—reaching an elevation of one hundred fifty feet.

All this had been created by a team of warm, friendly engineers and construction people who lived and worked there and wore uniforms much like Smokey the Bear.

Entering the plastic dome through two separate air locks we filmed the antenna as technicians explained its function to us: The antenna's job was to follow the satellite, Telstar, during a twenty minute window as its earth circling orbit carried it over the Atlantic Ocean. Because of the great distance between the antenna and the satellite a miss alignment of less than an inch would cause the antenna to miss the signal, so guess how exact the controls had to be. Having been a kid who always loved model trains I found the track and the giant base on which the antenna road fascinating.

As we filmed and talked we asked what news they had from the English and the French. We were told that the people there in

Andover were in daily contact with the British and, like themselves, the English antenna was working perfectly and all was in readiness for the scheduled July 23rd international telecast. As for the French... well, they had not heard much from the French. Our advisor/host was reluctant to say more.

In time—a couple of days—we completed our filming at Andover. Our New York film crew headed back to the Big Apple while John, Al and I prepared to go to England.

A brief side-bar here regarding our flight to London. Union contracts with the writers guild and the Radio and Television Directors Guild required first class transportation for John Apple and myself. NBC policy provided that when a Production Manager was traveling with a Director, he/she should have the same. I must admit I was not aware of that. Even if I had been it would likely have made no difference. First class air fare being more than double "tourist," I went to Reuven and asked if maybe NBC would provide two tourist tickets for me so that my wife could come with me. No Problem. It wasn't until we had all boarded our flight that Al Vechione laughingly told me I had cheated him out of his first, First Class trip to Europe. Since the director was traveling tourist, that was how the Production Manager would travel. Net result for NBC, the company saved half the cost of a first class ticket. (Well, I have always been very budget conscious.)

In London we were joined by a BBC Film Crew headed by cameraman Chris Callory, and a droll, very British sound man named Digby. Together with an electrician and an assistant cameraman, we set off for Goonhilly Downs Chris had been our cameraman in Holland and had become a friend. Having him with me again made the project even more wonderful in spite of the fact that he drove the car we were in and seemed determined to drive at the maximum speed he could achieve. Those gray hairs from Japan were joined by a fresh crop.

Somewhere along the way we stopped in a small village for a bite of lunch and Chris introduced us to "clotted cream." You could quickly grow fat on clotted cream but, my oh my, how delicious!

I think it was at lunch that Chris confided to us his dislike for automobile travel. The high speed resulted from his desire to get it over with as quickly as possible.

On to "Lands End" and "Goonhilly Downs." Not names that conjure up visions of warm, wonderful places and they are not. It was cold, foggy and wet when, silhouetted against the grey sky, the British antenna came into view. Unlike the cone shaped U.S. Antenna the English version was a round, inwardly curved metal skeleton standing uncovered at the top of a rocky hillside overlooking the Atlantic Ocean. Several hundred feet beyond the antenna stood a square, four story tall white building that housed the British control center. If you think the cold, grey sky looked uninviting, you should have seen that building.

We were welcomed by a very formal, uniformed officer. I believe the uniform was British Postal but looked very much like a navy uniform. We soon realized everyone on duty at the installation was in uniform; very polished, very British. We also quickly realized that many of the technicians were women. I could not recall any women at the U.S. site.

Once inside the building we were escorted to a viewing area that underlooked Control Central. I used the term "underlooked" rather than overlooked because four feet above the viewing floor where we stood, behind a three story high plate glass window, Control Central looked down on us. A long, narrow room housing a line of TV control panels, several of which were being attended to by technicians (all female) who were monitoring about two dozen TV screens. On most of the screens there was a still picture of Queen Elizabeth, on the others a picture of Big Ben. As the technicians punched different buttons the pictures switched. I immediately asked to go behind the glass wall into the control room where we could get close-up shots of the technicians working at their stations.

"I'm sorry, we can not permit that," our officer/host advised me. "That area is completely sterile. We could possibly outfit you people but your equipment would never be permitted."

So we took low angle pictures from the floor.

The three story high side of the building opposite control central held offices. Each office opened onto a railing enclosed walkway. (Looking at that layout I could not help but think of a prison where each cell opens out onto a walkway.) We did not have to be sterile to venture up onto the walkways, so we took hi-angle shots of the technicians at their work from each of them. From the third floor walk way we were also able to look out a window at the lonely antenna seated on the rocky hillside some distance away.

As we filmed, our officer/host gave us all sorts of information about the high level of British technical sophistication and occasionally suggested that we Americans were "right there with us" in many instances. Quite naturally, at one point or another, we asked about the French. Our officer/host pursed his lips once or twice before responding, then told us he really couldn't comment about that. We teased him a bit and finally got him to tell us, "Strictly off the record," that he did not believe the French would be ready or capable of participating in the historic telecast.

So, it was time to go to France.

While Johnny Apple and I were talking with our host and directing our film unit Al Vechione had been working. He had figured out it would be less expensive for us to charter a plane right there in Goonhilly Downs than for us to drive back to London, catch a plane to Brest, then fly a charter to Perros-Guirec. Way to go, Al! That is what Production Managers are supposed to do: Find ways to save money and time.

The airport at Goonhilly Downs was a bit of a surprise. As we pulled up to the airport building we thought there had been a mistake. The terminal was housed in a lovely, ivy covered building that looked more like a club house of some kind. Inside we were welcomed by a charming middle aged woman wearing a uniform of some kind and quickly escorted through the reception area out back to where an air plane sat awaiting us. Actually we did not realize the plane was awaiting us, we thought it was a museum piece from World War 1. A Bi-Plane with a single propeller engine. Before we had time to think much about it, dressed in a flying jacket, leather helmet and scarf around his neck, our pilot joined us. He welcomed us with great enthusiasm. He told us the plane… he mentioned the manufacture's name, I don't remember it but he assured us it was one of the safest airplanes in the history of aviation and he and the uniformed lady who had welcomed us were delighted to have the opportunity to take us on our journey to France. I really do not know why but for some reason we all just sort of nodded and climbed into the plane. As it turned out there were just enough seats for the eight of us. Our equipment and luggage was loaded into the aisle between the two rows of single seats—four on each side. A moment later our pilot somehow climbed over the stowed luggage and got to his cockpit. The door was closed, someone pulled the propeller down to start the engine and we looked out the window to see our uniformed lady waving a handkerchief at us.

"She was so hoping to come along," the pilot shouted over the roar of the engine, "But there just isn't enough room for her."

We began to move forward over a beautiful green lawn. As I looked out my window I realized one of the struts between the upper wing and the lower wing was not a cable. It was two lengths of rope, clothes line it looked like, tied in the middle with an 8-knot. Oh my….

As I thought about the rope we came to a stop. Looking beyond the rope strut I could see a long stretch of green grass. Rather a handsome runway, I thought. But why the delay?

"God Damn," I heard Johnny Apple say. He was seated on the opposite side of the plane. Looking out his window we could see a foursome of golfers approaching. Apparently the charter service made use of a golf club's fairway for its runway.

So we waited while the golfers played through.

Take off was uneventful. We easily cleared the trees surrounding the green at the end of the fairway but did not seem to gain much more altitude. As the flight progressed I came to the conclusion the plane was incapable of flight much above 500 feet.

Crossing the English Channel we flew over several islands. On one island a man—a farmer—was seated at a table in his back yard drinking a cup of tea (I assume) and reading his newspaper. As he looked up to give us a wave I could almost read the headline on the paper he was holding.

In time we arrived in France. We quickly cleared customs and took off again, this time for the French Telstar site near Perros-Guirec. Half an hour or so later we found ourselves circling a pasture. Several cows were contentedly grazing there. As we circled a man came hurrying out of the farm house alongside the pasture. He was carrying a large red and white checkered table cloth. He waved up at us then used the table cloth to chase the cows into a fenced yard thus clearing the pasture for us to land.

Taking off from a golf fairway, landing in a pasture, how bucolic can you get!

Perros-Guirec is a small, thriving resort city located on the English Channel in northern France. As we drove from our lovely hotel to the French antenna site the word "bucolic" fit the countryside perfectly. Low hills covered with small farms separated by wooded areas. Cresting one wooded hill and descending into a valley we could see a great deal of activity behind a road block ahead of us. As we stopped at the two saw horses blocking the road a well-tanned good looking young man, wearing a T-Shirt and jeans, came trotting towards us.
"You must be the television people," he shouted in very good but very French accented English. "Welcome. Welcome."

Beyond the road block, and the young man, was a sight I know we all remember. A massive excavation was being hand dug by twenty or more sweating men. Some wearing undershirts, most bare chested, all in coveralls or jeans. As part of the crew swung picks to loosen the soil, the others used shovels to load the loosened soil into saddle baskets slung over the backs of a string of donkeys. Yes, the four footed kind. Mules. Burros. I don't know how many, but there was a long line of them, and as the baskets were filled the donkeys went off up the hill to what I guessed was a dumping ground, then returned for another load.

"Come on, follow me," the young man called as he pulled one of the saw horses off the road so we could get by. He turned and waved us to follow him as he jogged down the road past a couple of wooden shacks to a picnic area where a half dozen or so tables and chairs were set out. "We have some fresh coffee," he told us. "Come."

Before I was even out of the van Chris Calory had a camera out and was hurrying towards the excavation and the donkey line. The place was truly a cameraman's dream.

Over coffee we spoke about the state of the American and British antennas and our surprise at finding the French just beginning construction.

There is a sound a Frenchman can make by blowing air past his lips. I cannot duplicate it, and I cannot accurately describe it, but it is a sound that says "phooey" better than any words. If you know a Frenchman you have probably heard that sound, if not, you have missed an entire vocabulary of derision in one sound. Our French friend made such a sound before adding, "Such a waste of time and money. The test is not for almost two months. We will be finished here in maybe four or five weeks."

Chris and I had a ball finding shots to make. Sweating brows, digging shovels, straining donkeys, an excavation growing larger every minute and nary a steam shovel in sight—just what decade were we in?

In time I noticed a small farm house nestled against the woods a half mile or so further down the valley. I asked about it and was told it was the home of the man who owns this farm. "He is not too happy that we took his land away," our host/guide told us. Well you know I wanted to interview him.

"Merde!" is one of the few French words I understand. It is a word that was frequently used by the young farmer as he and his wife told us how "They took our land." As he told it, the farm had been in his family since the time of Joan of Arc and "they" had just walked in and taken the land away. "Merde!!"

He did not mention receiving a large amount of money for the use of the land, nor the fact that the land would be returned to them once the Telstar program was completed.

So much for France. Well, not quite. There is a story I must relate.

Our stay in Perros-Guirec was at a charming, small resort hotel. I wish I could remember its name, but I can't. (Not important for this story.) The hotel featured a gourmet dining room. Table settings for each meal were exceptional, like nothing I ever experienced before nor have since. There were a dozen or more knives, forks, and spoons, each for use with a different dish: Hors D'Oeuvres, Appetizer, Soup, Fish or Chicken, Meat… on and on, course after course, and for each item a different utensil. Okay, you got the picture. So one evening as we were eating and trying to decided which knife or fork was appropriate we noticed Digby was not eating. Remember I mentioned Digby, our delightful, very British, very droll sound man. Someone, perhaps me, asked him if he was alright… if there was something wrong with his food.

"No," he told us, "I presume the food is fine but I do not have a proper fork for my fish."

I think someone threw a napkin at him but it wasn't me.

July 23rd found Ruth and me, along with a number of other people, in NBC Studio 8H in Rockefeller Plaza. We had been invited there to see the history making first trans-Atlantic telecast. President Kennedy along with RCA's General Sarnoff were standing by in Washington; Queen Elizabeth was ready in London; General de Gaulle reportedly in Paris.

The time arrived.

NBC Announcer (I think Ben Grower but some reports I have read indicate Chet Huntley and David Brinkley) told the audience, "Now, by satellite, we take you to London, England."

The TV Screen we were watching went dark. Then a bit of black and white static. Then dark again.

"We seem to be having a technical problem...just a moment... Already... Now, by satellite we take you to London, England..."

More black and white static. Then a sudden flash. For two or three seconds, the still picture of Queen Elizabeth, much broken up but recognizable as the one we had seen on the many screens at Goonhilly Downs.

Black screen again....then

OMG!!! The Arc de Triomphe with Maurice Chevalier and a line of 36 Bluebell Girls from the Lido, doing a production number right there on the Champs Elysees.

In my head I heard the very British voice of our Goonhilly Downs host mutter "Oh Shit!"

Time for a Change

REUVEN'S NEXT PROJECT was to be a documentary about Australia. He and I talked about the project but it involved moving to Australia for four or five months and I just did not see myself leaving Ruth and our boys for that long. Somehow I found a job as Associate Producer for "Loveable Louie," a pilot project Ed Sullivan's company was developing for a half hour series about a monkey in training to become a space monkey.

(Side note: Reuven Frank continued to climb the NBC staircase and wound up President of NBC News some years later.)

Time now to re-introduce Ted Rogers.

Perhaps you are wondering what happened to Ted. Well Ted was always like a rubber ball, no matter how far he dropped, he always bounced back. About the time I finished work on Telstar and went to work for Ed Sullivan's company, a man named John Kluge was negotiating to buy The Ice Capades from creator John Harris. Kluge was an enormously successful entrepreneur who had built a Washington DC drug store into TV Giant, MetroMedia. For reasons unknown to me Kluge had decided to expand his TV giant into the world of live entertainment and his first acquisition was The Ice Capades, which he purchased from John Harris in the summer of 1963 for a reported $5.5 million. And who do you suppose John Kluge hired to head up MetroMedia's live entertainment division? Sure, you knew it all the time, none other than the bouncing ball, Ted Rogers.

So, a few weeks after I started on "Loveable Louie" I got a phone call from Ted telling me of his good fortune and asking if I would be interested in a job with Ice Capades. I remember half laughing as I told him I did not know the difference between a hockey puck and a hockey stick and I didn't think the ice world was the place for me. As fate would have it, "Louie" was not either. The idea was great, the script was wonderful, but finding a midget to play the space monkey was turning into a joke. Not a funny joke. So as September was turning into October and the hunt for a Louie was becoming more and more frustrating, Ted called again. Would I reconsider Ice Capades. He and Kluge had decided a good way to break many of the company's long held ties with John Harris would be to move company headquarters from Hollywood to New York. This would mean no move to California for my family and me. So, how 'bout it? I told him I would talk it over with Ruth.

"How much longer will 'Louie' last?" Ruth wanted to know.

"Couple-a-months, maybe a bit more." I told her.

"Then what?"

Well, damn it, I didn't have an answer for that. So I called Ted and said yes.

Life On Ice

AS I LEFT the Ed Sullivan Office on West 57th Street for the last time one of the secretaries, sitting at a desk I was passing on my way to the elevator, began to cry. "Don't cry," I chuckled as I pat her shoulder. "We'll meet again."

"No... It's the president..." It was November 22nd. President Kennedy had just been shot.

It is generally conceded that everyone old enough to know what was happening in the world on that day remembers exactly where they were when they first heard the news. Certainly I do. I was in a state of shock as I took a taxi cab to Idyllwild Airport (now JFK) for a plane to Las Vegas where I was to meet Ted and people from Ice Capades. It was during the flight that we learned the President had died. Certainly not an auspicious beginning of a new life for me. But the omen of bad fortune turned out to be incorrect.

My wonderful life with Ice Capades is probably worth a book by itself but for this opus I am going to relate only two stories which have nothing to do with ice skating:

ICE CAPADES national tour began in September each year at New York's Madison Square Garden and ended at the Los Angeles Coliseum just after Memorial Day. Then, each summer, right after the 4th of July, executives, skaters, and the entire company moved to Atlantic City, New Jersey, where we set up shop in the old Atlantic City Convention Hall. Rehearsals were held and preview performances of the "new" show presented. The summer of 1964 was my first visit to Atlantic City.

Wanting our first edition of Capades to be something extra special, we brought in Sid Smith, a well know TV Director, to create a wonderful, new show and Sid, in turn, engaged Sid Kuller who Wikipidea identifies as:

"an American comedy writer, producer and lyricist/composer, who concentrated on special musical material, gags and sketches for leading comics."

It was probably the day after Sid Kuller checked into our Convention Center offices that he and I went out to lunch together.

A short walk from the Convention Center a large, rather impressive (for AC) building housed the 500 Club as well as a restaurant named the "Beef and Beer." The 500 Club proudly proclaimed itself as a home for Frank Sinatra and the place where Dean Martin and Jerry Lewis began their careers. The Beef & Beer was a great place for lunch. Sid said he wanted to go to there to see the owner, his old friend Skinny D'Amato who, as I later learned, not only owned the Beef and Beer but the 500 Club and the building in which they were located. Sid had known Skinny since writing material for a Martin and Lewis appearance at the 500 Club. We had lunch and Skinny D'Amato joined us. I do not recall what we discussed that day and Sid Kuller never told me very much about Skinny D'Amato other than the fact that they had worked together on a couple of Martin and Lewis acts as well a Duke Ellington TV Special. The three of us had lunch once or twice more before Sid returned to Hollywood and Skinny and I became casual friends.

Shortly after Sid left, before I knew anything about Skinny, he asked me to join him for lunch one day. He was a great baseball fan, as was I, so our conversation was mostly about the New York Yankees. As we were talking, a waiter bearing a telephone approached our table. (This was long before the days of cell phones and mobile devices.) He bent over a said something to Skinny who took a resigned breath, said "Sorry about this" to me, then picked up the phone and answered the caller. As a good guest I tried to pay no attention to what Skinny was saying but after a moment his voice became louder and I could over hear what he was saying whether I wanted to or not.

"No! You cannot have Frank Sinatra.," he told the caller. "You have Patti Page and she will do just great for you." With that, he hung up.

I am sure my eyes widened and blinked once or twice as I began to realize something about the influence wielded by the man I was having lunch with.

The following summer (1965) I brought a film crew down from New York to shoot material for TV Commercials. The crew checked into the motel next door to the Convention Center and put their equipment van in the parking garage. Next morning the van was empty. Cameras, Lights, Film; all missing. After a fruitless morning of telephone calls to the Atlantic City Police I took a break and went to the Beef and Beer for lunch. I found a table and almost before I sat down Skinny joined me and asked if I was alone and could we have lunch together.

"How's your day goin?" he asked.

"Not good," I said and told him about our minor disaster.

He expressed disappointment over having something like that happen to us in Atlantic City and said he would see if there was anything he could do to help. He suggested after lunch I go back to my office and stay close to the phone. About an hour later that phone rang and a somewhat muffled voice told me if we would look over at the corner of (two streets I do not remember) we would find what we were looking for.

And there, with a police officer standing on the opposite corner, sort of looking the other way, there, carefully laid out on the sidewalk, was every last bit of our equipment, including a half used roll of adhesive tape.

Later that summer we were taping our yearly TV Special. The

show always featured one or two Special Guest Stars and that summer, fresh from the success of her recording "These Boots Are Made For Walking," Nancy Sinatra was one of them. At lunch with Skinny one day he said he had heard we were taping the show and that Nancy was going to be on it. He asked when would she get to town. I told him yes, she was on the show, we had taped her yesterday and she had left last evening.

A look of sad disappointment came over Skinny's face. As I think back it was a look very much like the look on Jackie Kennedy's face when she spoke of being lonely.

"Gee," he said softly. "She's my God Daughter and she didn't even call."

My final Skinny D'Amato story does not really involve Skinny. It starts way back in the Gillett Cavalcade of Sports days. In those days there was a close relationship between Gillette, Madison Square Garden, the International Boxing Club and NBC Television. The Friday Night Fights from New York's Madison Square Garden were a major, weekly telecast for NBC so, not surprisingly, boxing stories were always an important part of the Gillette Sports Review I was working on. Visits to training camps and interviews with top boxers were frequent and usually arranged through an IBC public relations man named Joe Roberts.

If memory serves me correctly it was at Heavy Weight Champion Rocky Marciano's training camp, at or near Grossingers Resort in New York's famous Catskill Mountains, where I first met Joe. He was a heavy set man probably in his 40ies, almost never without a cigar in his mouth. Joe had a rather loud, gravelly voice and, much to my annoyance, he always called me "kid." Well, I was a kid—24 years old when we first met—but his calling me that always rankled. "Hi kid, what-cha need today?" That was Joe Roberts. But in spite of "kid," Joe and I became sort of friends and he was really quite a guy. I remember him once telling me about buying a new car. I asked "what kind?" He said he wasn't sure—he needed a new car so he went to the first dealership he came to and bought one. He said he didn't care what kind of a car it was because he knew all American cars were built great. (That really was a long time ago!!!)

Now a few words about the International Boxing Club for which Joe worked:

IBC was a corporation formed in 1949 to promote prize fights at Madison Square Garden as well as a number of other prime locations throughout the country. It developed a stranglehold on championship boxing. Between 1949 and 1955 IBC promoted 47 out of the 51 championships fights that took place in the U.S. In 1960, during the famous "Kefauver Hearings" into organized crime, it was revealed that IBC had ties to the Mafia's Frankie Carbo.

Skip forward now to 1968, Montreal, Canada: "EXPO '67, was the World's Fare held in Montreal in 1967. Expo 67 had been such a success it was held over for a second year and became EXPO '68. For reasons not all together clear to me, Ice Capades decided to try out a non-skating show there and as a result I spent a good bit of time in Montreal that summer. It was there, at the end of August, when I next heard from Ted Rogers.

I had not talked with Ted in a long while and I'm not sure I even knew he was no longer with Metro Media. In any event I quickly learned he had joined Hugh Hefner's Playboy Organization as head of live entertainment which, at the time, consisted mainly of entertainment presented in the Playboy Clubs. Ted had learned I was in Montreal and called to ask if I could do him a favor. Playboy was considering a business relationship with the owner of one of the largest nightclubs in Montreal. For some reason Ted could not get to Montreal at the moment and asked if I would go have diner at the club, meet the owner, see the stage show being presented there and report my reaction to the club's operation. Needless to say, I said yes. Free meal, good show, why not?

I think singer Don Cornell was the headliner that Tuesday evening. Whether or not he was, the show was excellent; the food even better and, perhaps best of all, having dinner with the club's owner was fun. We exchanged meaningless stories about each other then got into baseball. My host was an ardent Red Sox fan. "My God, you remind me of Skinny D'Amato," I laughed, "Except he's a Yankee fan."

"Jesus, do you know Skinny?" my host asked. As I nodded yes he added. "We argue about baseball every time we get together." He went on to tell me Skinny was one of his best friends and he was going to Atlantic City next day to meet Skinny and together they were going to Florida for a couple of weeks of Bone Fishing.

That same week "Capades" ended its AC run and was heading for Madison Square Garden in New York City, and on Thursday I left Montreal for New York and the Grand Opening of our new show. As part of the hoopla for the opening of each new edition, Ice Capades hosted an Annual Arena Managers Convention there in NYC. As one of the hosts for the convention's Friday night welcoming cocktail party I was exuding charm and friendship as I greeted guests when who do you suppose walked in? Slightly older, but not much different in looks, cigar still firmly clinched between his teeth, you guessed it, none other than "Hi-ya kid, " himself, gravel voice Joe Roberts.

"What-cha doin' here?" Joe wanted to know.

I told him of my association with Ice Capades and asked him what he was doing here. I knew IBC had closed up shop some years ago but supposed Joe still had some arena connections. "Just passin' through," he told me with a couple more "kids" thrown in, on his way up to Canada. "Really," I told him, "I just got back from Montreal," and wouldn't you guess, that was where Joe was headed. He told me he had some ideas he wanted to talk over with a guy who runs a big night club up there.

I asked him if by any chance he was talking about the owner of the club I had visited. Joe's face expressed surprise. He asked if I knew him. I told him "yes," I'd had dinner with him three nights ago, then added, "You're out of luck. Joe. He and Skinny D'Amato are headed to Florida for some bone fishing."

Joe took the cigar out of his mouth and a moment of stunned silence. Then, in a much different tone of voice from any I had ever heard before, he asked me if I knew Skinny D'Amato. "Sure," I said. "We spend every summer in AC and Skinny has become a friend."

Joe blinked once or twice then, in an even more different tone of voice asked, "Phil, can I buy you a drink?"

I can't leave my Skinny D'Amato story without a bit more information regarding the man and his connection with Frank Sinatra. Sinatra started playing in Skinny's saloon in the 1950ies when his wild affair with Ava Gardner nearly brought his career to an end. With Skinny's help, and his own great talent, Sinatra re-built his career and continued to play there well after his Oscar-winning return to prominence. He would often work the club just for expenses. While filming "The Pride and the Passion" in Spain, he sent Skinny a telegram that read, "How about August 24, 25, 26, 27?" It was signed "El Dago." Skinny had the telegram framed and hung in his office.

(Ah-ha! That's why he wasn't in Madrid when I went there to film material for HOME. Well, hell, I'd rather have a date with Sophia Loren anyway. And besides, I had already played cards with Bing Crosby. Who needed another singer?)

When Skinny was named Atlantic City Man of the Year in 1982, Sinatra chaired the event. When Skinny was buried in 1984,

Sinatra was a pall bearer. It may have been at the Kefauver Hearings that Sinatra was asked if he knew any Organized Crime Family members. He is reported to have answered, "Sure. I work in nightclubs and most of them are owned by crime family members."

Wikapedia identifies Skinny D'Amato as:

> *Paulino D'Amato ran the rackets in Atlantic City for the Genovese Family. He owned the 500 Club which was a Front for an illegal gambling operation. To draw gamblers the club booked top acts, Frank Sinatra, Martin & Lewis and many more. Sinatra became a very close friend and was a pall bearer at Skinny D'Amato's funeral in 1984.*

I never worked in a nightclub but I did work in the entertainment industry and I too knew a few Family Members. I did not know them well, I did not know Skinny D'Amato well—nothing of his Mafia activities—to me he was simply a kind and helpful friend.

The Magic Screen

AS JOHN KLUGE and Ted Rogers re-shaped the Ice Capades organization they selected George Eby, a man who had been the company treasurer, to be President of the new organization. It was perhaps the best decision the two men ever made together. George Eby was a man of great ability, patience, charm and kindness. He brought together the old and the new and built an organization that was really quite exceptional.

My first meeting with George was in Las Vegas on that fateful November 22nd. Over the ensuing years George and I became good friends and frequently visited Las Vegas together. No, not at all what you may be thinking, we went there on business. Las Vegas was a wonderful place to find talent and show ideas. One of the "tasks" I had to undertake as part of my duties with Capades, usually together with George, was to visit entertainment centers here in the U.S. as well as in Canada and much of Europe, in search of show ideas and talent. (It was a tough job but someone had to do it!) Vegas was a prime spot. At least three times a year we went there and stayed at the Tropicana Hotel—which at the time was the newest hotel on the strip. Unlike other hotels on the strip, the Tropicana Show Room did not present Big Name entertainers of the Frank Sinatra; Liberace; Martin and Lewis ilk, instead the "Trop" featured a somewhat Americanized version of the famous French "Follies Bergere," a show that featured beautiful, scantily costumed girls and top specialty acts.

On one visit—January or February, 1956 I believe—George and I were enjoying the show as an act "in one" finished. ("In one" meaning the act performed on the stage apron in front of the main curtain.) As the act left the stage, the curtain opened to reveal a motion picture screen and a film of a group of ten or twelve dancers performing on the impressive steps of a court house or state capital type building. Then, as the dancers came down the steps they suddenly stepped off the screen to materialize, live, in the flesh, right there on the stage above us. WOW! The act was called "The Magic Screen," and magic it truly was. George and I knew an act like that we gotta have!

Tropicana entertainment director and friend Maynard Sloat, quickly arranged a meeting for us with the man who had created the act and we negotiated a contract with him. For the next three years Mr. Magic Screen (as I shall refer to him for a while) and I worked together for a month or two each year preparing a Magic Screen act for Capades and, as you might expect, we became pretty good friends. But, as often happens in show biz, when our contract with him was completed we lost touch with each other, and not long after that I left Capades to join David Wolper's company and get back to film making and television.

The "lucky man" designation was never more appropriate than when I went to work for David Wolper. Television was using more and more film projects: Series, Movies made for TV, and documentaries. And Wolper's company was a leader in the field. Within a few months after joining, David and Alex Hailey got together to create and produce "Roots." My job as Production Manager opened doors to projects that kept me busy for the rest of my working life.

In 1979 my wife, Ruth, died. Some lonely years followed.

One day George Eby and I were having lunch. (It had been a dozen years since I left Capades but George and I had remained good friends and made it a practice to get together at least once a month or so.) George asked me if I remembered Shirley Winter—a beautiful former star of Capades who had become Skating Director for the Ice Capades Chalets. Yes, I remembered her, she and I had met several times back in the days when I was with the company. George said he had run into her recently and learned she was also alone....

Shirley and I were married in 1988.

Home for us was basically Los Angeles but Shirley had a long time love affair with Carmel, California and owned some property there. The Monterey Peninsula is one of the most beautiful places in the world and as she and I visited there more and more frequently we wound up buying a home in Pebble Beach. As the 1990ies approached we were gradually becoming peninsula residents, living there much of the time. When I had a film project in the works down in LA, thanks to United Airlines, I spent most weekends with Shirley in Pebble Beach.

As I am sure you realize by now, my memory for dates is not always too good. However, sometime towards the late 1980ies my old Magic Screen friend's name began turning up in show biz magazines and newspapers and even in columns in the New York Times. He was becoming known as an International Entrepreneur. And somewhere about that time we heard he and his family were also living here on the peninsula. "You should look him up," Shirley often told me but being the foot dragger I am, I did not. Then, one Monday morning, when Shirley was dropping me off at the Monterey airport, we pulled up behind a car with a familiar name on the license plate. I told Shirley to wait a minute or two and perhaps she would finally get her wish. As I got out of the car, emerging from the terminal building and heading for the car with the familiar license plate; there, together with his lovely wife Lee, came Mr. Magic Screen himself. The license plate read "TIBLEE" and Mr. Magic Screen was Tibor Rudas who was becoming world famous as the producer of spectacular concerts by Luciano Pavarotti.

In the years since then Lee and "Tiby" have become close friends, and over the years I have learned a great deal about Tibor Rudas. Not from him—he is not given to talking about himself—but from his son, Dean, who has become something of a nephew to Shirley and me.

Shortly after the end of World War One, Tibor was born into a poor Jewish family living in Budapest, Hungary. He was a talented and precocious youngster and as a child of five or six was singing and dancing on street corners in return for the Hungarian version of nickels and dimes. As it happened, the Rudas Family lived near the Budapest State Opera House and, consequently, Tibor's performances were on nearby street corners.

In those days the state opera conducted a school for talented youngsters. Someone from the opera saw Tibor performing and he received a scholarship to the state run school which, in addition to special training in singing, dancing and performing, taught everything from what we call "kindergarten" all the way through college, with special attention to the business of entertainment.

Tibor was an excellent student who excelled at acrobatics and dance. By the time he became a teen-ager, in addition to appearing regularly in the opera chorus and dance ensembles, he had brought together a couple of classmates and formed an act which played professionally in clubs and theaters in Budapest. A happy future in entertainment seemed assured, but dark clouds were forming over Hungary.

Hungary had been allied with Germany during WW1 and the tie between the two governments had not broken. As Hitler and the Nazi party grew to power in Germany their influence on Hungary became more and more apparent. In 1938, in a country that for years had prided itself on its Jewish population, Hungary passed the first laws restricting what businesses Jews could run, what jobs they could hold. Then in 1941, as German invasions took over Europe, Hungary rounded up all Jews and sent them to forced labor, concentration camps. The camp Tibor was sent to, and the labor he was forced to do, was entertain Hungarian troops and government officials. This he did for a number of years. But not much lasts forever.

Not long after D-Day, the invasion of Normandy, Tibor found himself jammed into a railroad cattle car along with literally dozens of others—too crowded to lie down or sit, maybe you could squat. That night the train began to move, slowly, with many stops, then just before dawn the train made another stop but did not move again. After several hours of waiting some of the men managed to pry open one of the boards in the side of the car. They were able to make an opening large enough for a slender acrobat like Tibor to get through. Once outside the car, being careful to keep hidden as much as possible, Tibor took a look around. He could see no soldiers, no train crew, no one, nothing. As he explored further, above the low moaning coming from the cattle car, he began to hear a mechanical sound. As it grew louder he realized something was approaching. He hid under the car, watched and waited. Off in the distance an object appeared. In a moment he could see it was a tank, then another and another. As they got closer, son Dean told me, Tibor could see the tanks were flying American Flags. (I have checked Google's history book and cannot find any indication American Forces ever invaded Hungary but regardless of that the tanks were "good guys.")

After being freed, in time, as a refugee, Tibor made his way to England then on to Australia where he settled and opened a school for performing arts. With his best students he created an acrobatic dance group that became enormously popular in Australia. The act, "The Rudas Dancers," was seen by Follies Bergere scouts and brought to the Tropicana Hotel where he soon created "The Magic Screen."

For some years Tibor and wife Lee lived in Las Vegas where their children were born and, in addition to the Magic Screen and the Rudas Dancers, where Tibor developed other acts that played in hotel show rooms in Canada, Chicago and the Bahamas. Then in 1978 he was offered a job as Entertainment Director for the newly opened Resorts International Hotel and Casino in Atlantic City, New Jersey.

Once a major beach resort (and Mafia controlled illegal gambling and prostitution center) Atlantic City had fallen on hard times. In 1976 New Jersey decided to legalize gambling in the hope the city and the state's fortunes could be revived. Resorts International was the first of several grandiose casino hotels to open in Atlantic City and Tibor was given a virtually limitless budget with which to bring Top Name entertainers to AC in order to lure patrons away from Las Vegas. And Tibor did a very good job. Resorts International became very successful. Then, one day—must have been in the early 80ies—Tiby told management he had signed Luciano Pavarotti for a two week stay in the main show room. Management's reaction to this announcement was not good. It was something like, "The opera singer? You gotta be kidding! We don't want no opera singer here." Tibor told management he had already signed a contract with Pavarotti and management told Tiby, "You signed him, you pay him and keep him out-a here!"

Tibor took a deep breath, borrowed all the money he could, put up a huge tent with a stage and 5,000 seats and announced Pavarotti's coming appearance. Advance ticket sales were astounding. So much so that Tiby took the first money in and spent it to have the tent enlarged and an additional 2,000 seats installed.

For Pavarotti's two week stay every show was a sellout. Along about the fourth day Resorts Management came smiling to see Tibor. "We never should have doubted your genius," they told him, and they wanted him to bring Pavarotti into the main showroom for as long as he wanted.

"Thanks fellows," Tiby replied, "But Luciano and I have other plans."

The "other plans" included concerts in arenas and outdoor venues all over the world. A performance for the Royal Family and half a million enthusiastic fans at Hyde Park, another half million in New York's Central Park. Then, the creation of The Three Tenors—Jose Carreras, Placido Domingo and Pavarotti. The Three tenors made an indelible mark on the face of modern entertainment.

And that is my story of a poor boy who made good.

Only a few months before I began this opus Lee Rudas passed away. Today Tiby is a sad and lonely man. Shirley and I share his grief and extend our love to him.

P.S. September 8, 2014: Word just received today from Tiby's daughter, Kim. Her father passed away this morning. Tiby and Lee are re-united now, and those of us remaining here wish them great joy for ever and ever.

Final Thoughts

AS I PROOF READ THIS I find myself thinking about the many successful people I met who began their lives in what we like to call, "modest circumstances:"

United States Senator Margaret Chase Smith started working at age 12 in her father's barber shop helping shave her father's customers.

Carl Sandberg. School dropout at age 13 to get a job driving a milk wagon. Working as a hotel porter, a brick layer.

Rocky Grazziano. School dropout growing up in the crime ridden lower east side of New York.

Robert W. Service. Sent to live with his aunt at age six.

Kate Smith. Speaking difficulties as a child, parental disapproval of her wanting to sing.

Sophia Loren. A street waif wounded by shrapnel during World War II.

Tibor Rudas. Singing and dancing on street corners at age 5 or 6.

All these people overcame youthful problems, poverty, lack of education, but with talent, ambition and diligence each achieved unbelievable success.

I believe there is a lesson here for each of us.

Postscript

My Writing Career

WRITING, or trying to write, has been a hobby of mine since I was old enough to do it. When was that? Second Grade? Maybe Third? When does a youngster have enough learning to know how to make letters into words? We were still living on Staten Island, land of my birth, so it had to be before I was nine when I made my first attempt.

One of my next door neighbor friends and I decided to publish "The Randal Manor News." A newspaper dealing with events in our two square block area of the world. Our major accomplishment as newsmen came about one afternoon when we were coming home from school. A neighbor lady was driving her car down the steep driveway to the garage under her house. The garage door was closed but she did not stop and went right through it.

"Extra. Extra."

The Randal Manor News was on the street in less than an hour. By that time a reporter from the Staten Island Advance (the major paper on Staten Island) was at the accident scene. Proudly we gave him a copy of our paper. Was that a scoop or was that a scoop?

It was a lot of years later, really after more than 25 successful years in Hollywood, when my beloved Shirley and I "retired" to our Pebble Beach home, that I seriously concentrated on writing and I have published three books to show for it. Each fiction, each an outgrowth of my life's experiences.

The first two, "Staten Island," and "Hollywood's Best," deal with what I believe is the strong tie between the world of entertainment and organized crime.

Let me make clear what I consider "organized crime" to be.

In my mind crime organizations, whether it be the Mafia or some other group, exist not for the purpose of holding up banks and killing people but primarily to make money providing illegal entertainment for the thousands, make that millions of people who seek it. Back in "the 20s," when the United States declared Prohibition, our most famous criminals made fortunes selling illegal beverages. Think Run Runners ruling the seas and Bootleggers clogging the highways. Think Al Capone. Think Speak Easies doing turn away business. And one of the primary attractions at Speak Easies, in addition to booze, was music and entertainment. Well known night clubs grew up in cities across the country. Famous orchestras and performers were featured as were the clandestine teacups full of Rye, Scotch, or Bourbon. Or perhaps Gin—I believe the Martini was invented during Prohibition times. And Hollywood grew to maturity in the years before WW2. This is the background for "Staten Island," and "Hollywood's Beat."

A change of direction for my third book. "Final Assignment," is the story of today's world. The story of a TV News Cameraman who's camera is also a weapon capable of undetectable homicide. His victims have been ordered by the President of the United States… or have they?

Book Number 4: "Lucky Man."

And now I am done.

Now there must be time for us to pause a moment
        Here together in the afternoon.
And so we sit fondly gazing at each other
        Thinking of the day just passing.

Softly come the shadows.
        But so slowly we are not aware.
There is no change, not for us,
        It happens all too gently for our senses to perceive.

Then, suddenly, some distance off, a light is lit.
        New. Bright. Shining.
We see it clearly, though it is far, far away..
        Only now do we realize the darkness that has found us.

It seems come too quickly, yet it is here.
        But being here together, we are not afraid.

Phillips Wylly

The End